WHAT TOP ADs, COACHES, AND ATHLETES ARE SAYING . . .

"Jeff Janssen's work with our student-athletes through the Michigan Leadership Academy has been tremendous. His ability to communicate with our student-athletes, along with his ability to draw student-athletes into deeper discussions about leadership is outstanding. We are fortunate to work with Jeff and experience firsthand the way he gives student-athletes insight into how they think, how they perceive, how they process, and how they can become great teammates and performers."

JOHN BEILEIN, MICHIGAN MEN'S BASKETBALL COACH

"Jeff's programs have huge value and his resources are extraordinary. I have learned so many things from Jeff and so have my players and teams."

ANSON DORRANCE, LEGENDARY WOMEN'S SOCCER COACH, 22-TIME NATIONAL CHAMPIONS

"I loved *Championship Team Building*. It is obvious that Jeff has done a great deal of work on the subject of team building."

MIKE KRZYZEWSKI, DUKE MEN'S BASKETBALL COACH

"I've been in the business for over 30 years and there are a lot of different programs I've seen. What the Janssen Sports Leadership Center does is the best out there. It builds on itself. It is not a one-time seminar. You will see a change in student-athletes in terms of leadership on the field, in the classroom, and everywhere else."

JEFF LONG, COLLEGE FOOTBALL PLAYOFF SELECTION COMMITTEE FIRST CHAIRMAN

"Not only did I grow up as an athlete but also as a person through Jeff's Leadership Academy. The Leadership Academy taught each participant how to better handle difficult situations and how to effectively communicate with teammates. Furthermore, the Leadership Academy allows athletes to have in-depth discussions with athletes from other teams fostering a championship mentality for all participants. Lessons I learned from Jeff not only made me a better leader on the field but also helped prepare me for the corporate world. Jeff's passion and spirit is unparalleled and he truly listens to every single athlete to help the situation at hand. I cannot describe how thankful I am for my experience with the Leadership Academy and I will continue to look to Jeff as a mentor."

KARA CANNIZZARO, WOMEN'S LACROSSE NATIONAL PLAYER OF THE YEAR (HONDA SPORTS AWARD)

"Jeff is an amazing motivator and a truly g   ener. He challenged the student-athletes at the University of Illinois to become gr   agined, not just in their sport, but in life. He also encouraged us to giv   ity and to be the self-less and courageous leaders that would   ountry, and the world. Jeff's passion and commitment   mitable. He has had an immeasurable impact on so ma   n many of us the confidence to succeed, the willingness to do mo   needed for life."

CECE MARIZU,   MEN'S SWIMMER

For more info on the Janssen Sports Leadership Center visit www.JanssenSportsLeadership.com

ADDITIONAL RESOURCES BY JEFF JANSSEN

BOOKS

The Team Captain's Leadership Manual: The Complete Guide to Developing Team Leaders Whom Coaches Respect and Teammates Trust

The Team Captain's Culture Manual: The Complete Guide to Working with Your Team Leaders to Develop a Championship Culture

How to Hold People Accountable Manual: The Complete Guide to Establishing, Endorsing, and Enforcing Your Team's Standards

The Athlete's Responsibility Manual: The Complete Guide to Developing Responsible Athletes Who Reliably Get the Job Done

The Athlete's Commitment Manual: The Complete Guide to Creating Committed and Compelled Athletes

How to Build and Sustain a Championship Culture

Championship Team Building: What Every Coach Needs to Know to Build a Motivated, Committed, and Cohesive Team

Jeff Janssen's Peak Performance Playbook: 50 Drills, Activities & Ideas to Inspire Your Team, Build Mental Toughness & Improve Team Chemistry

The Seven Secrets of Successful Coaches: How to Unlock and Unleash Your Team's Full Potential

How to Develop Relentless Competitors

Develop Relentless Competitors Drillbook

The Mental Makings of Champions: How to Win The Mental Game

WEBSITES

Team Captains Network—www.TeamCaptainsNetwork.com

Championship Coaches Network—www.ChampionshipCoachesNetwork.com

**For more info on the Janssen Sports Leadership Center visit
www.JanssenSportsLeadership.com**

THE
TEAMMATE'S
ACCOUNTABILITY MANUAL

The Complete Guide to Developing Athletes Who Deliver Results Rather Than Excuses

HOW TO BE AN ACCOUNTABLE TEAMMATE

ACCOUNTABLE ATHLETE

Keep Your Commitments and Deliver Results

Own Your Responsibilities and Role

Have Your Teammate's Back

Recognize Your Ripple Effect

Eliminate Excuses

Consider the Consequences

Accountable 2U

© JanssenSportsLeadership.com

JEFF JANSSEN

This publication is designed to provide accurate and authoritative information in regard to the subject matter covered. It is sold with the understanding that the publisher is not engaged in rendering legal, accounting, or other professional services. If legal advice or other expert assistance is required, the services of a competent professional person should be sought.

Published by Winning the Mental Game
6841 Piershill Lane, Cary, NC 27519
Phone: 1-888-721-TEAM
Email: jeff@jeffjanssen.com
Website: www.janssensportsleadership.com

ISBN 978-1-892882-22-6

DEDICATION

To Anson Dorrance
Thank you for the opportunity to learn from you and your amazing
North Carolina women's soccer program! You have taught me so
much about leadership, motivation, responsibility, accountability,
competitiveness, and what it takes to build and sustain a
Championship Culture. Thank you for the difference you have made
in my life and so many of your amazing players!

SPORTS LEADERSHIP DEVELOPMENT SERIES

Our popular Sports Leadership Development Series provides athletes, coaches, and athletic administrators with a practical, progressive, and proven sports leadership development training program that spans a student-athlete's entire career. The comprehensive curriculum targets student-athletes at their specific level of leadership development. The series starts with teaching the critical self leadership skills of responsibility, accountability, and commitment and then progresses on to the more advanced skills of effective team leadership building a championship culture, and holding teammates accountable. So no matter where your athletes might be in terms of their personal leadership development, you'll have the appropriate level of training for them.

Level 1: Personal Responsibility—*The Athlete's Responsibility Manual*
The Athlete's Responsibility Manual trains student-athletes how to take full responsibility for themselves by owning their choices, decisions, and actions. The six-module program is geared for all freshmen to complete as early as possible during their first year—or as a great summer read before they start school.

Level 2: Team Accountability—*The Teammate's Accountability Manual*
The Teammate's Accountability Manual shows athletes how their attitudes and actions significantly impact their teammates' and coaches' success and failure. This six-module program extends and expands on the material in Level 1 and can be done with all freshmen in the first semester of their first year.

Level 3: Commitment—*The Athlete's Commitment Manual*
The Athlete's Commitment Manual trains student-athletes how to completely commit to their task, training, and team through the use of the powerful Commitment Continuum™ tool. This six-module program can be done with all freshmen in the second semester of their first year.

Level 4: Team Leadership—*The Team Captain's Leadership Manual*
Designed for emerging team leaders, *The Team Captain's Leadership Manual* is a 10-module leadership development program that trains athletes how to be effective Leaders by Example and Vocal Leaders. Use it early on with your sophomores who demonstrate leadership potential.

Level 5: Championship Culture—*The Team Captain's Culture Manual*
Designed for established team leaders, *The Team Captain's Culture Manual* teaches captains how to best partner with the coaches to build and sustain a Championship Culture in your program. Use this 10-module, advanced leadership development program with your junior and senior team captains.

Level 6: Holding People Accountable—*How to Hold People Accountable Manual*
Designed for respected team leaders, the *How to Hold People Accountable Manual* teaches and trains your leaders how to effectively hold their teammates accountable to your team's standards and core values. Use this 8-module, advanced program with your senior team leaders.

For more info on the Sports Leadership Development Series visit
www.JanssenSportsLeadership.com

TABLE OF CONTENTS

COACHES' INTRODUCTION AND GUIDE

"The first challenge in constructing a Championship Culture is to make them accountable. Almost every discussion I have with freshmen goes back to being accountable. One of the hardest things to establish in any culture is to make sure everyone is accountable."

Anson Dorrance, North Carolina Women's Soccer Coach

"There are three things we can't have. We can't have complacency, we can't have selfishness, and we can't lose our accountability."

Nick Saban, Alabama Football Coach

"Responsibility equals accountability equals ownership. And a sense of ownership is the most powerful weapon a team or organization can have."

Pat Summitt, Legendary Tennessee Women's Basketball Coach

"The most important quality I look for in a player is accountability. You've got to be accountable for who you are. It's too easy to blame things on someone else."

Lenny Wilkens, Hall of Fame NBA Basketball Coach

Accountability. Clearly all coaches desperately want and need it from their athletes but so few of them consistently have it. Unfortunately being fully accountable for your actions is a dying art in today's world. We live in a society where too often parents and people allow and sometimes encourage kids to avoid being accountable. They excuse them, coddle them, find loopholes for them, fight their battles for them, and accept their lame and laughable excuses thinking somehow they're helping their kids—they're not. Not now—and especially not long term. Simply watch ESPN for just a few minutes and you will see numerous situations and stories of entitled athletes failing to be accountable for their actions.

CODDLING VS. COACHING

Athletes who understand and act on what it means to be fully accountable are tougher to find. More and more of today's athletes (and their parents) expect to be coddled rather than coached. Coddling caters to athletes' wishes and whims, keeps them in their comfort zone, accepts excuses, tolerates selfishness, and diminishes accountability. If coddled athletes don't get what they want, they sulk, pout, and complain to their parents and administrators or switch teams/schools until they can find someone who will give them exactly what they want. Coddling obviously softens athletes and creates lazy, fragile, entitled, moody, excuse-making jerks.

Effective coaching, on the other hand, sets high expectations, pushes athletes out of their comfort zone, and holds them accountable to meet the necessary standards to be successful. Effective coaching creates strong, hard working, mentally tough, resilient, and accountable athletes.

Accountability then is paramount not only for a successful sports team—but for a successful life.

Here's one of my tweets @janssenleader that resonated with thousands of coaches:

THIS IS WHY . . .

- I COACH YOU because I care about you.

- I CHALLENGE YOU because I believe in you.

- I EXPECT YOUR COMMITMENT because I know your family and job will.

- I HOLD YOU ACCOUNTABLE because I know life will hold you accountable.

You know that to develop successful people for the Game of Life, it is your responsibility as a coach to teach your athletes what it means to be accountable—first to themselves and their teammates—but eventually to their own family and coworkers because you know that's what life will demand from them when they are future parents and professionals. Sooner or later, life will hold them accountable. That's exactly why this Accountability Training Program was created.

The Teammate's Accountability Manual provides you with a practical and proven six-week system for teaching your athletes the critical life skill of accountability. There are many who preach the importance of accountability but very few systematically teach it. So, just as you teach your athletes sports skills, they also need to learn, practice, and *apply* what it means to be a trusted teammate and how to be completely accountable to one another.

WHY USE THE TEAMMATE'S ACCOUNTABILITY MANUALS

The Teammate's Accountability Manuals will help you develop a Culture of Accountability within your program. For your program to be successful, your athletes must be accountable to themselves, their teammates, your coaching staff, and numerous others who make up your program. By teaching your athletes exactly what it means to be accountable, giving them meaningful activities, evaluations, and practical ways to practice being accountable each week, and having them work with an Accountability Partner to ensure follow through, you provide them with the essential insights, structure, and skills to be accountable.

WHO: Because everyone needs to be accountable to each other, you can do the program with your whole team the first year you implement it. Once you have the foundation in after Year 1, you can then run it with your freshmen after completing *The Athlete's Responsibility Manual.*

WHAT: To build your athletes' accountability, this program will help them learn, practice, and master the 6 Attitudes and Actions of Accountable Teammates: 1. Own Your Responsibilities and Role, 2. Recognize Your Ripple Effect, 3. Consider the Consequences, 4. Eliminate Excuses, 5. Have Your Teammate's Back, 6. Keep Your Commitments and Deliver Results

WHEN: *The Teammate's Accountability Manual (Level 2)* ideally should be implemented after your athletes complete *The Athlete's Responsibility Manual (Level 1)*, as the two resources complement and build off of each other. The best time to start the Accountability Training Program is in your offseason or as early in your preseason as possible and run it over six weeks. You can obviously continue the basic elements of the program once the foundation is in place.

HOW: The best way to use *The Teammate's Accountability Manuals* is to provide one for each of your athletes and pair them up with a different Accountability Partner (AP) each week. An AP is a fellow teammate who will help them define their weekly tasks and responsibilities, provide them with valuable support and feedback throughout the week, and hold them accountable to keep their commitments and deliver results. The first meeting should be used to introduce the program, pair up your athletes with an AP, and have each AP list their Top

5 to 7 Tasks on their Accountability Partner Weekly Feedback Sheet on page 18. During the week the athletes should then read and complete the chapter and regularly check in with their AP to hold them accountable. Change their APs each week so they get to team up with six different teammates. Dedicate anywhere from 20-40 minutes each week to implement the program, ideally at the beginning of the week, before the start of practice when your athletes are still fresh. A rough agenda includes:

5-10 Minutes: Have the previous week APs rate and discuss each other's accountability during the past week using the questions from the chapter and the bottom half of the Accountability Partner Weekly Feedback Sheet.

10-20 Minutes: Discuss how the ideas and strategies from the chapter relate specifically to your team. Have people discuss their insights, evaluation ratings, Top 3-5 Takeaways, and Top 3 Teammates who best demonstrate the theme of the week located at the end of each chapter. If your team is young or somewhat immature, you or one of your staff members can facilitate the weekly discussion. Or, if you have a more veteran or mature group, you can break up your team into smaller groups, assign them chapters to prepare for, and hold them accountable to facilitate the discussion with the rest of their teammates.

5-10 Minutes: Athletes meet with their new AP to discuss their Top 5 to 7 Tasks for the current week and come up with a fun/challenging/measurable challenge to encourage them to do it.

(If you really want to go in-depth with this and have enough staff to assist, you can implement a version of Coach Jerry Kill's Warrior Elite Program. Here you assign athletes or have them draft teammates on to Accountability Teams. Accountability Teams are then awarded points when their teammates fulfill their weekly responsibilities and deducted points when they don't. The team with the highest point total gets special privileges and the one with the lowest point total often has penalties. More details can be found at www.teamcaptainsnetwork. com/public/362.cfm or in our *How to Build and Sustain a Championship Culture* book.)

Thanks again for investing the time and effort to teach your athletes all about accountability! Not only will you set them up for success on the playing fields, but for the game of life as well!

HOW TO BE A GREAT TEAMMATE

Being a great teammate can best be understood by this simple yet powerful equation:

$$\frac{\begin{array}{c}\text{Responsible 4Me}\\ \text{x} \quad \text{Accountable 2U}\end{array}}{\text{GREAT TEAM8}}$$

A GREAT TEAM8 adopts the mindset: I am completely Responsible 4Me as well as fully Accountable 2U. Simply put, you earn your teammates' and coaches' trust by taking full responsibility for yourself and solidify it each and every time you demonstrate your accountability to them. When you live by, train by, and compete by this equation, you not only make a HUGE contribution to your team's success, you also earn your teammates' and coaches' utmost respect as a GREAT TEAM8, a truly priceless treasure. Let's break down each of the components of this important equation so you know how you can powerfully impact your team.

Responsible 4Me

Being a GREAT TEAM8 starts with being completely responsible for yourself. Responsible 4Me means taking 100% ownership of every one of your daily

© JanssenSportsLeadership.com

choices, decisions, and actions. When you act this way on a consistent basis, you earn your teammates' and coaches' trust. *The Athlete's Responsibility Manual* focuses on what it takes to be completely responsible for yourself and your behavior.

Accountable 2U

Being a GREAT TEAM8 also means being fully accountable to your teammates and coaches. Accountable2U means you understand how your attitudes and actions intricately and indelibly impact your teammates' and coaches' success and failure. Because you recognize the Ripple Effect your behavior creates, you consciously and consistently choose attitudes and actions that contribute to and benefit the whole team—not just yourself. Every time you and your teammates are accountable to each other, you multiply the respect and trust amongst your teammates and create a Championship Culture of respect, reliability, and loyalty in your program. The *Teammate's Accountability Manual* focuses on what it means to be 100% accountable to your teammates and coaches.

GREAT TEAM8

Finally, when you consistently act in ways that demonstrate you are fully Responsible 4Me and Accountable 2U, you earn your teammates' and coaches' confidence that you can and will consistently do what is best for the team, have their backs during the tough times, and thus become a highly respected, reliable, loyal, trusted, and GREAT TEAM8 in their eyes.

Responsible 4Me

x   Accountable 2U

GREAT TEAM8

ATHLETES' INTRODUCTION AND GUIDE

"Being there every week for my teammates is really important to me. It's about accountability."

Peyton Manning, Two-time Super Bowl Champion

"There's responsibility, but there's also accountability. You have to be accountable for your actions."

Derek Jeter, New York Yankees

"You have to hold people accountable. If you want to win sometimes you have to have a difficult conversation with people."

Carla Overbeck, U.S. Soccer Women's National Team

"Everybody is going to have to be accountable. If you're on the field, you have to give me 100 percent. Always. We have to weed out the bad seeds, point blank. If you can't give me what I'm giving you on the field, I don't need you on the field with me. I have no problem telling that guy I don't need him on the field, and I have no problem going to tell Bill (Belichick) I don't want him on the field. That's how you win."

Vince Wilfork, New England Patriots

"I thrive on the accountability of a group environment. . . . Marathon running is all about consistency—whatever you put into it you're going to get out of it. So having someone or a group is essential for training. Finding a running buddy or running group to help keep you on task I think that really makes or breaks someone's preparation."

Shalane Flanagan, New York City Marathon Champion and Three-time Olympian

Accountability. As you can see from the quotes above, athletes and coaches want it and all teams need it if they are going to be successful. But what exactly is a Culture of Accountability, how do you create and sustain one within your program, and what kind of benefits does being more accountable to each other bring to you and your team?

Welcome to *The Teammate's Accountability Manual*! This six-week Accountability Training Program, designed specifically for athletes, will help you and your teammates understand exactly what it means to be accountable to each other and how critical accountability is to building a Championship Culture.

When you are on a team, you must be 100% accountable to your teammates and coaches. In fact, accountability is one of the most important factors that differentiates an actual TEAM from a mere group of people. While a group is just a collection of individuals, a TEAM has a common goal and a sacred commitment to be fully accountable to each other for achieving that goal.

When you think of the words accountable or a Culture of Accountability, what comes to mind?

_____

_____

_____

Let's first define what we mean by a Culture of Accountability.

A Culture of Accountability is one where people mutually depend on and hold each other accountable to fulfill their roles, keep their commitments, eliminate excuses, have each other's back, and consistently deliver winning results that benefit the entire team.

A Culture of Accountability is one where teammates and coaches:

- value achieving results and consider them essential for team success

- value relationships based on mutual respect and trust

- clearly understand and abide by the desired results, standards, and expectations of the team

- realize that everyone's success, failure, and reputation is interconnected

- understand the consequences and problems they cause others when they don't do their job

- feel they let down the team if they don't do their job

- refuse to offer or tolerate lame excuses for a lack of performance or results

- have their teammate's back through good times and bad, especially the bad

- keep commitments to each other and know their word is their bond

- hold people accountable for living up to the team's standards and delivering results

- recognize, reward, and promote people who meet and exceed standards and deliver results

- clarify, correct, coach, and demote people who fail to meet standards and/or deliver results

- eliminate people who become a significant drag or distraction or violate nonnegotiables

In a Culture of Accountability, people realize, respect, and relish the fact that they are answerable to each other and the entire team. Teammates and coaches willingly step up and do what needs to be done with little prodding or complaint because they take responsibility for and pride in playing their role and value the chance to contribute to a cause greater than themselves. The team, in turn, acknowledges and appreciates them when they successfully fulfill their responsibilities and admonishes them when they don't. The more everyone buys into this kind of mutual accountability the less anyone ever wants to let down their teammates.

OPPOSITE OF ACCOUNTABILITY—CULTURE OF EXCUSES

Another way to understand a Culture of Accountability is to contrast it with its polar opposite: a Culture of Excuses. In this kind of lazy and lame culture, people spend significantly more time and energy finding excuses than finding a way to get the job done. They would rather play the Blame Game or get caught up in the futile and vicious Victim Cycle.

In a Culture of Excuses, teammates and coaches:

- blame others for a lack of results

- ignore or deny their accountability—saying "It's not my job"

- hope the problem or situation resolves itself or magically fades away

- wait for others to tell them what to do rather than taking initiative

- cite confusion or poor communication as reason for inaction and failure

- come up with excuses why they can't do or achieve something

- profess they are helpless, that they couldn't do anything about it (victim mode)

In a Culture of Excuses, people relinquish responsibility for their actions and abdicate their accountability to others. They feel powerless and let the situation and others dictate their success rather than taking responsibility for the things they can control.

Obviously there is a HUGE difference between a Culture of Accountability and a Culture of Excuses. A Culture of Accountability attracts and retains winners and a Culture of Excuses repulses and repels them. The dramatic difference between the two cultures not only substantially impacts your team's chances of success but also determines your team's culture and how much you enjoy being around your teammates and coaches.

Having the amazing opportunity to work with and learn from over 30 NCAA National Championship teams from a variety of schools and sports, I've discovered that a Culture of Accountability revolves around these six essential Attitudes and Actions of Accountable Teammates:

6 ATTITUDES AND ACTIONS OF ACCOUNTABLE TEAMMATES

1. Own Your Responsibilities and Role

2. Recognize Your Ripple Effect

3. Consider the Consequences

4. Eliminate Excuses

5. Have Your Teammate's Back

6. Keep Your Commitments and Deliver Results

When these six elements are firmly in place with your team, you too can create a powerful Culture of Accountability in your program that drives and supports your success, builds a culture of respect, and attracts and retains trusted and talented teammates.

Each chapter of *The Teammate's Accountability Manual* highlights each of these six important areas by providing you with several practical and proven strategies, stories, skills, and surveys to learn and master these areas.

How to Use and Benefit from the Teammate's Accountability Manual

This six-week Accountability Training Program teaches and trains you how to hold yourself accountable so others don't have to. Becoming more accountable will gain your teammates' and coaches' respect and trust, help you earn more playing time by consistently delivering winning results, contribute significantly to your team's success, enhance your program's reputation, and provide you with critical skills that will help you the rest of your life.

Work with Your Accountability Partner to Hold Each Other Accountable

The best way to learn accountability is to practice being accountable to each other on a daily basis. So each week you will partner up with an Accountability Partner (AP) on your team so you can help each other, support each other, coach each other, and ensure that both of you do what your team needs you to do to be successful.

It is up to you whether your team wants to call them Accountability Partners, Battle Buddies, Support Sisters, etc. The key is that you will have at least one teammate who you are fully responsible for motivating, supporting, and making sure they follow through on their weekly commitments to this program, their training, their assignments, and the team. They in turn will do the same for you. You will be there for each other and hold each other accountable to do what needs to be done, when it needs to be done, and at the level it needs to be done to benefit yourselves and the team.

To help guide you in this process, you will be challenged to discuss and share with your AP your primary responsibilities and tasks each week that need to be accomplished for your and the team's success using the top half of the AP Weekly Feedback Sheet. See the example below:

ACCOUNTABILITY PARTNER WEEKLY FEEDBACK SHEET

My Responsibility/Role/ Expectation/Job This Week:	Impacts Whom?	Positive/ Negative Consequences?	Due Date?	Results Delivered?
Complete chapter in Accountability Manual	me/team/ coach	let team down, run	10/10	<u>Yes</u> or No
Write and turn in English paper before trip	me/team/ coach	lose 50 pts, study tables	10/11	Yes or <u>No</u>
Remember to call Mom for her birthday	Mom	make Mom's day	10/14	<u>Yes</u> or No
Watch video on upcoming opponent	me/team/ coach	help our team win	10/15	<u>Yes</u> or No
Improve free throws (make 5 in a row daily)	me/team/ coach	win more games	10/16	<u>Yes</u> or No

Column Key:

My Responsibility/Role/Expectation/Job: What specific things do you need to do or accomplish this week that will affect or impact your teammates and coaches in some way?

Impacts Whom? Consider all the specific people your actions impact either positively or negatively if you do or don't do them.

Positive or Negative Consequences? What are the positive or negative consequences and outcomes that will likely happen if you do or don't do your job?

Due Date? By exactly what date and time do you need to have this task fully completed?

Results Delivered? Did you do what was expected/needed? Did you deliver results?

AP CHALLENGE

You can even create a challenge between you and your Accountability Partner relating to your responsibilities and tasks during the week to sweeten the pot a little bit. For example, let's say your AP wants to work on her free throws because she is only shooting 65%. You can challenge her to make at least 8 out of 10 free throws after practice. You can place a friendly reward or consequence on it of carrying her gear, buying her a coffee, or something else that you both mutually agree upon. If she completes it you owe her and if she doesn't, she owes you.

You will also be asked to provide your AP with some valuable feedback by rating them. The key is to be candid and constructive with each other in your feedback. Many times people can lack self-awareness of how they come across to their teammates and coaches so your honest feedback will help them better understand how their actions impact others and how well they do their job. You will then coach them, support them, and hold them accountable on how well they demonstrate accountability to their team responsibilities, expectations, commitments, and roles during the week—and they will do the same for you. Near the end of the week, set a time to meet and go over the material from the chapter. There is an Accountability Partner Feedback Sheet to complete and discuss each week.

Throughout the week you can check in with each other and hold each other accountable. You can do this when you see each other on campus, at lunch, in the weight room, at practice, etc. At the end of each week, you will also be asked to rate your AP on the 6 Attitudes and Actions of Accountable Teammates each week.

1. How well did your Accountability Partner own his/her responsibilities and role this week?

2. How well did your Accountability Partner recognize his/her Ripple Effect?

3. How well did your Accountability Partner consider the consequences before acting?

4. How well did your Accountability Partner eliminate excuses?

5. How well did your Accountability Partner have your back?

6. How well did your Accountability Partner keep their commitments and deliver results?

In addition to working directly with your AP each week, ideally your team will also get together to discuss the strategies in the chapter and how they apply to your team as a whole. You and your AP will be expected to fully participate in and contribute to these discussions. If either of you is not prepared or contributing to the discussion, your teammates and coaches will hold you *both* accountable, as they should.

RATING YOUR CURRENT LEVEL OF ACCOUNTABILITY

As we start the program, take a moment to honestly rate yourself on your current level of accountability using the 6 Attitudes and Actions of Accountable Teammates Self Eval on the next page. Your ratings will help you see your current strengths and help you pinpoint specific areas where you might need to improve.

6 ATTITUDES AND ACTIONS OF ACCOUNTABLE TEAMMATES EVALUATION

This evaluation helps you see how accountable you are to your teammates and coaches. Honestly answer the questions using the 1 (Strongly Disagree) to 10 (Strongly Agree) scale below.

1–2 = Strongly Disagree
3–4 = Disagree
5–6 = Neutral
7–8 = Agree
9–10 = Strongly Agree

1. **Own Your Responsibilities and Role:** I clearly understand, accept, and own my team responsibilities and role and competently and reliably fulfill them to the best of my ability.

   1   2   3   4   5   6   7   8   9   10

2. **Recognize Your Ripple Effect:** I recognize and respect the fact that my actions and attitudes affect and impact the success and reputation of my teammates, coaches, and others.

   1   2   3   4   5   6   7   8   9   10

3. **Consider the Consequences:** I consciously and carefully consider the consequences of my words and actions on my teammates, coaches, and others before I speak and act.

   1   2   3   4   5   6   7   8   9   10

4. **Eliminate Excuses:** I refuse to make excuses by blaming someone or something else for my mistakes, failures, and losses. Instead, I claim full accountability, apologize, analyze, and fix it.

   1   2   3   4   5   6   7   8   9   10

5. **Have Your Teammate's Back:** I am always there for my teammates and coaches, especially through the tough times, and do not gossip about, undermine, or betray them in any way.

WEEK

1

   1   2   3   4   5   6   7   8   9   10

6. **Keep Your Commitments and Deliver Results:** I keep the commitments I make to my teammates and coaches and consistently deliver the high-level results they expect from me.

   1   2   3   4   5   6   7   8   9   10

Add up your total score for each of the six questions:

TOTAL SCORE _____

6 Actions of Accountable Teammates Evaluation Rating Scale

54–60— You are a highly Accountable Teammate! Teach your teammates what you know.

46–53— You are somewhat accountable with some room for improvement. Study this Manual.

38–45— You are not as accountable as you and your team need you to be. Take a lot of notes.

30–37— You are not accountable and can benefit greatly from completing this Manual.

6–29— You are a highly unreliable teammate! Memorize and apply this Manual!

Your self evaluation is a good place to start your journey to becoming a more Accountable Teammate. In addition to rating yourself, you should also strongly consider having your coach and Accountability Partner rate you as well. These additional perspectives can be especially helpful because people often positively skew their self ratings.

How does your coach rate your current level of accountability?

Coach Score: _____

How does your AP rate your current level of accountability?

AP Score: _____

Odds are, in many cases, your coach and AP will likely have a slightly to significantly lower score for you—and see some areas where they would like you to improve your accountability. Rather than taking this difference of opinion personally and becoming frustrated or upset by it, use their helpful and more objective feedback to focus on and improve the specific areas and chapters where they think you could become more accountable as an athlete, student, and person.

Thank you for going on this journey to greater accountability. Not only will it help you individually, but it will also make a big contribution to your team as well. Let's get started!

ACCOUNTABILITY PARTNER WEEKLY FEEDBACK SHEET—MODULE 1

Accountability Partner Name: _____

Date: _____

What exactly is expected/needed of you and how can you best contribute to the team this week?

My Responsibility/Role/ Expectation/ Job this Week:	Impacts Whom?	Positive/Negative Consequences	Due Date?	Results Delivered?
				Yes or No
				Yes or No
				Yes or No
				Yes or No
				Yes or No
				Yes or No

AP Challenge: _____

(Which task can you put a fun/measurable consequence on with your AP if you deliver results?)

At the end of the week, have your Accountability Partner rate you on how accountable you were:

1. How well did he/she own and execute his/her responsibilities and role this week?

    1   2   3   4   5   6   7   8   9   10

2. How well did he/she recognize and respect his/her Ripple Effect?

    1   2   3   4   5   6   7   8   9   10

3. How well did he/she consider the consequences on others before acting?

    1   2   3   4   5   6   7   8   9   10

4. How well did he/she eliminate excuses?

    1   2   3   4   5   6   7   8   9   10

5. How well did he/she have your back as your Accountability Partner?

    1   2   3   4   5   6   7   8   9   10

6. How will did he/she keep his/her commitments and deliver results?

    1   2   3   4   5   6   7   8   9   10

Comments:

_____

_____

_____

_____

CHAPTER 1

OWN YOUR RESPONSIBLITIES AND ROLE

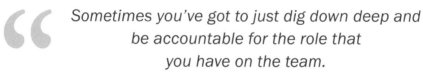

Sometimes you've got to just dig down deep and be accountable for the role that you have on the team.

Julius Peppers, NFL Player

The first step to being accountable to your teammates and coaches is to clearly understand and abide by the responsibilities and role you need to fulfill for your team's success. As an Accountable Teammate, you must know, accept, and fully own what your teammates and coaches need and expect from you as a contributing member of the team. It is difficult if not impossible to be fully accountable to people if you don't understand exactly what they want and need from you. So it is critical to learn, know, and clarify your responsibilities and role on the front end, which we will do in this chapter.

BE ACCOUNTABLE FOR FULFILLING YOUR RESPONSIBILITIES

Let's start with your responsibilities. As a member of the team, there will be certain responsibilities you will need to fulfill to contribute to and demonstrate your commitment to the team. These responsibilities are often outlined by the rules, standards, and expectations that your team has to be a productive member of the team. While sometimes they are written down and clearly explained when you join the team, unfortunately most times it is assumed you will just naturally learn your responsibilities from observing your more experienced teammates and by trial and error over time. Rather than leaving this important aspect to time and chance, take the initiative to identify and learn your responsibilities and what is expected of you on the front end.

Be sure to clarify with your coaches and teammates exactly what actions and attitudes they expect of you to be a contributing member in good standing with your team. Be clear about what is acceptable and unacceptable to do as a member of your team. Most teams will obviously have a set of rules and standards they hopefully communicate to you at the beginning of the season and require you to abide by when it comes to your behavior. These typically include expectations for your behavior for practice, the weight room, classroom, social media, social life, on road trips, etc. Here is a great example of Iowa State Football's Cyclone Code of Conduct:

- I can always be heard saying PLEASE when asking for something.

- When given something, I always say THANK YOU.

- Likewise when someone says thank you, I will say YOU'RE WELCOME.

- To politely interrupt, I will say EXCUSE ME.

- I can always be heard saying YES SIR, NO SIR or YES MA'AM, NO MA'AM to my parents, my instructors, coaches, advisors, managers, trainers, etc.

- Phrases such as : GOOD MORNING, BE SAFE, HOW ARE YOU and HAVE A GREAT DAY are all part of who I am.

- I AM THE RESPECTFUL CYCLONE!

Clarify Exactly What's Expected of You So You Can Be Fully Accountable for It

Why is clarifying your responsibilities so important? You can't be accountable to your team for fulfilling these expectations if you aren't crystal clear about what is expected. So it is up to you to seek them out and for coaches and captains to clearly communicate and clarify them on the front end.

Not being clear about your expectations would be like me telling you, "Meet me in Texas." Obviously this is way too broad of a statement (and state) and nowhere near specific enough for you to find me. You could go to El Paso next week and think you fulfilled your responsibility only to discover that's not what I had in mind. If I clarified it a bit more and said, "Meet me in Dallas," it would narrow things down significantly, but still not be super helpful for you. If I said, "Meet me at the Dallas/Fort Worth airport outside of Gate A23 at 12:00 pm on January 1 of this coming year," you would know exactly where to go and when to be there. I could reasonably expect and hold you accountable to meet me there at that exact time and place because I specifically communicated where I wanted you to meet me and when. Without clear expectations both communicated and understood, accountability is impossible. Thus, if you are going to hold yourself or someone else accountable, you must have a crystal clear understanding of exactly what is expected.

Discussing Responsibilities vs. Dictating Responsibilities

In today's world, how your coaches and team leaders communicate your expectations and responsibilities is going to have a much better chance of being fulfilled if they discuss them with your teammates rather than dictating them. Dictating responsibilities means the leader just tells people what to do with no rationale, discussion, or questions. It is one-way communication that discounts the opinions, attitudes, or questions of the listener. It basically says you must act this way or else. When responsibilities and expectations are dictated from coaches and/or captains with no rationale behind them, people are less likely to buy in to and own those responsibilities as their own. Worse, they are often less likely to abide by them are actively resist them.

Conversely, discussing responsibilities means that you have dialogue with your teammates about the responsibilities, what they mean, why they are important, and how they are helpful and necessary to your team's success and a key part of your culture. Discussing responsibilities gives people a chance to see the reasoning behind the expectations, ask questions about them, clarify what they mean, understand their value, and create better buy in to them. When helping people understand your team's responsibilities, invest the time to discuss them with the team rather than dictate them.

Clarifying responsibilities allows teams to clearly establish and communicate their expectations and standards in a variety of areas so everyone on the team understands the behavior to which they will be held accountable. The following exercise helps you better discuss and clarify your teammates' responsibilities in a variety of areas so that you are clear about what is acceptable and unacceptable for you and others to do.

> "The single biggest problem in communication is the illusion that it has taken place."
>
> **George Bernard Shaw**

TEAM RESPONSIBLITIES AND EXPECTATIONS

The specific responsibilities and expectations I need to consistently abide by and fulfill as part of being a contributing member of this team include:

Practice Responsibilities and Expectations

What actions are acceptable and expected at practice?

_____

_____

_____

What actions are unacceptable and not tolerated at practice?

_____

_____

_____

Academics Responsibilities and Expectations

What actions are acceptable and expected when it comes to academics?

_____

_____

_____

What actions are unacceptable and not tolerated when it comes to academics?

_____

_____

_____

WEEK
1

Weight Room Responsibilities and Expectations

What actions are acceptable and expected in the weight room?

_____

_____

_____

What actions are unacceptable and not tolerated in the weight room?

_____

_____

_____

Fitness/Conditioning/Diet Responsibilities and Expectations

What actions are acceptable and expected when it comes to fitness, conditioning, and diet?

_____

_____

_____

What actions are unacceptable and not tolerated when it comes to fitness, conditioning, and diet?

_____

_____

_____

Social Life Responsibilities and Expectations

What actions are acceptable and expected in your social life?

_____

_____

_____

What actions are unacceptable and not tolerated when it comes to your social life?

_____

_____

_____

Social Media Responsibilities and Expectations

What actions are acceptable and expected when it comes to social media?

_____

_____

_____

What actions are unacceptable and not tolerated when it comes to social media?

_____

_____

_____

Campus and Community Responsibilities and Expectations

What actions are acceptable and expected on campus and in the community?

_____

_____

_____

What actions are unacceptable and not tolerated on campus and in the community?

_____

_____

_____

Being an Accountable Teammate means understanding these responsibilities, accepting these responsibilities, and owning these responsibilities each and every day. These expectations are obviously in place so your team can consistently perform at its best, build a productive culture, and represent your team in a positive way. Your team needs you to be responsible for acting in these ways and accountable to each of your teammates for abiding by them.

(To further help clarify your team's standards and expectations, check out our Standards of Behavior section in our _Team Captain's Culture Manual._)

If you can't consistently be accountable for meeting these expectations and responsibilities you:

- hurt your team's chances of success

- lose your teammates' and coaches' trust and respect

- damage your and your team's reputation on campus and in the community

- jeopardize your status and playing time on the team

It is obviously critical that you fulfill your responsibilities to contribute to your team and earn and maintain your team's trust and respect. While investing the time to clarify responsibilities and expectations on the front end is critical, you will also need to remind each other about these throughout the season. You can also provide each teammate with a copy of these responsibilities so everyone has them. You can post your Team Responsibilities in the locker room and weight room as continual reminders of your expectations. The visible reminder also makes it easier to hold people accountable to them because they are clarified in black and white so there should be no confusion or misunderstanding about them.

KNOW, ACCEPT, AND OWN YOUR ROLE

In addition to your responsibilities as a team member, being an Accountable Teammate also means you will be assigned and expected to play a specific role for your team's success. Keep in mind you were recruited to or selected for this team for a particular reason. The leaders of the team wanted you to be a part of it because they believe you have a current or developing skill set that can contribute to the team's success. You bring certain things to the team that are crucial for its success. Most of the time, your skill set is a physical one related to your sport skills, but you can also bring a valuable skill set of being a great leader, teammate, motivator, communicator, organizer, etc., that also contributes significantly to your team's success.

By playing this role, you do your part in helping the entire team be successful. Much like each particular piece contributes to putting together a larger puzzle, your individual role is necessary to complete your entire team's success.

Obviously some roles like the starting quarterback, pitcher, striker, leading scorer, etc., are often perceived as more glamorous and receive more attention from the fans and media, yet each role is an important and valuable one for the team's success. There are many highly valuable behind-the-scenes roles that are essential for a team's success, though the general public may not be aware of them.

> "Believe in your role. Stay in your role. Star in your role."
>
> **Doug Collins, NBA Coach**

3 STEPS TO FULFILLING YOUR ROLE

There are three steps to effectively fulfilling and executing your role to best help your team:

1. Know Your Role

2. Accept Your Role

3. Own Your Role

Step 1: Know Your Role

The first part of being accountable to your team for your role is to completely understand it. To play your role effectively you must invest the time to clearly understand what is expected of you. After a reasonable number of practices and competitions, many coaches will set up individual meetings with each of their athletes to discuss the specific role they feel the athlete will play for the team's success. If your coach does this, use this as a good opportunity to understand fully what your coach wants and needs from you. Ask questions so that there is little confusion about what your current role might be. Be sure to end the meeting by summarizing what you heard the coach say regarding your specific role on the team to ensure clarity.

KNOW YOUR ROLE. ACCEPT YOUR ROLE.
OWN YOUR ROLE.

Keep in mind that most roles are not fully formed until competitions have started and coaches have been able to see how you and your teammates perform and respond in competition situations. Be patient as your particular role evolves within your team. Your coaches will likely need at least a handful of competitions to occur before they have a better feel for what your role will be. Further, it is also critical to understand that roles can and often do change during the season. Obviously someone on your team might get hurt, leave the team, or get into a performance slump. These typical occurrences often necessitate a change in roles for some members of your team. Understand this is a normal part of a season and be able to make the adjustment when called upon, which brings us to the next step.

On a scale of 1 to 10, how clear are you about your current role on the team?

1   2   3   4   5   6   7   8   9   10

How would you describe your current role and what your team needs from you? (If it is too early in the season to fully know your role, list how you think you can best contribute to the team.)

_____

_____

_____

Step 2: Accept Your Role

Once you clearly understand your role, your next step is to accept it. Obviously this is much easier to do if the role you are given by your coach is the one you want. Most athletes obviously want to start, play the premier positions, get a lot of playing time, and be appointed the team captain. When you earn and receive these roles they are certainly easy to accept.

However, keep in mind that a large segment of your team will not be assigned their ideal role on the team. Many of you will be reserves, some will feel like they are out of position, others will want a more coveted spot, others feel they should be a captain, etc. Further, you may have been a starter in previous seasons and now find yourself on the bench because a younger player is getting more playing time at your position. It is all part of being on a team. If you are not a starter or playing the perfect position you would like, odds are you are not going to like your role. This is certainly understandable. However, for the time being, you need to accept and respect your coach's viewpoint on your role and play it to the best of your ability.

Even though it may not presently be your ideal role, you need to learn to accept it and respect it. Notice I didn't say you had to LIKE your role. Just because you may not like your current role doesn't mean that your teammates and coaches don't need you to play it and play it well. They still rely on you to play your role to the absolute best of your ability. You don't have to like your current role—but you do need to accept it as it is now for the good of your team.

On a scale of 1 to 10, how well have you accepted your current role?

  1   2   3   4   5   6   7   8   9   10

Accepting your current role means you will:

_____

_____

_____

How to Expand Your Current Role If You Don't Like It

The best way to expand your role is to play it so well that your coach sees you are ready and able to take on a bigger role for the team. As the saying goes, "Be so good they can't ignore you." This means being able to consistently deliver key results as we will discuss in the sixth chapter.

> "I can't complain about playing time.
> My job is to play so well the coach can't sit me."
>
> **Shane Battier, NBA Player**

Even superstar NFL quarterbacks Aaron Rodgers, Tom Brady, and Dak Prescott began their careers as back up role players. Rather than complaining about their situations and low position on the depth chart, they made the absolute best of their opportunities by working hard, studying and mastering the playbook, talking with the coaches, and learning from and supporting the starter in front of them. Even though they didn't like being a "benchwarmer," they accepted their current role, played it well, and when they eventually earned their opportunity to play, they were ready for it. You too will likely get a chance to expand your role at some point either through an injury to a starter or because you have improved your skills so much and delivered such consistent results in practice that your coach wants to get you in the competition.

It is usually okay to respectfully and occasionally ask your coach what you might need to do to earn an expanded or different role in the future. Find out specifically what skills and results your coach wants or needs more of from you and then work with your coach to devise a training plan that helps you develop and improve in these areas.

Step 3: Own Your Role

Owning your role means fully embracing it and making a commitment to yourself and your teammates that you will play your role to the absolute best of your ability. If your job is to be the long snapper for your team, you commit that every one of your snaps is going to be at a high quality. If your job is to be the bullpen catcher, you commit to playing that role and preparing your team's pitchers to be at their best. If your job is to play the #6 spot in tennis, you commit to competing intensely and winning a point for your team.

Owning your role means fully investing in it, taking pride in it, and being 100% accountable for it. You will do whatever is necessary to fulfill your role at the highest level possible and that your team can fully rely on you to consistently get the job done. When you approach your role with this kind of admirable at-titude, your teammates and coaches take notice, and look to find an expanded role for you whenever possible.

Google "Kyran Ashford", a Southwest Airlines worker who marshals the planes on the tarmac at the Rochester International Airport. While most people see the job of guiding the planes in and out of the gate as a menial and mundane task, Kyran has completely owned his role and taken it to a whole new level. His exuberant dance moves while guiding the planes have been a huge hit with passengers and have gone viral. Kyran's goal of giving passengers "30 seconds of positive vibes" has gotten him noticed around the world and by his employers— showing that he is ready, willing, and able to serve in bigger ways. No matter what your role might be, you too can do it at a masterful level and fully own it.

> "If a man is called to be a street sweeper, he should sweep streets
> even as a Michaelangelo painted, or Beethoven composed music,
> or Shakespeare wrote poetry. He should sweep streets so well that
> all the hosts of heaven and earth will pause to say,
> 'Here lived a great street sweeper who did his job well.'"
>
> **Dr. Martin Luther King, Jr.**

On a scale of 1 to 10, how well have you fully owned and embraced your current role?

1   2   3   4   5   6   7   8   9   10

Owning Roles Leads to Rings

While everyone knows LeBron James, far fewer know of his teammate, Tristan Thompson. However Thompson has played a key role in helping LeBron and their fellow teammates win an NBA Championship by knowing, accepting, and owning his role. Thompson only averages a mere 8 points a game compared to LeBron's 30—but Thompson's key contribution and role for the Cavs is rebounding and defense. Thompson averages over 8 rebounds a game, which typically leads the team. These often unnoticed rebounds are essential to Cleveland's success and has helped them win a championship. Thompson says, "I try to be the best I can be at what I can do, and that's playing hard and rebounding." He may not get the same attention as LeBron, but they both have the same championship ring.

Do Your Job

New England Patriots coach Bill Belichick, who has led the team to several Super Bowl Championships, has always had one simple yet powerful motto— Do Your Job. Obviously Do Your Job is a succinct way of saying that each player needs to fully know, accept, and own his role. Coach Belichick says, "I think in terms of our players and our team, each of us has a job to do, and the only thing that we can do is do the best that we can. That's improve on a daily basis, work hard, pay attention to the little details, and put the team first. So whether it's myself, a player, or an assistant coach, it doesn't really matter who it is, we all can only do what we can do. And we try to do that in team context, and try to work as hard at it as we can and improve on a daily basis.

Patriot wide receiver Danny Amendola adds his take on the "Do Your Job" motto and mantra as well. "To me, personally, 'Do Your Job' is everybody has a role on this team, no matter what it is. I like to think of it like our team is kind of like a car. Some guys might be the motor. Some guys might be the windshield wipers, the lights, steering wheel. Other guys might be like the lug nuts or something, but the car's not going to run if you don't have the lug nuts on. No matter what it is, you've got to do your job." As Amendola says, whether you are the lug nut on your team or the motor, every single part of the car is essential and must execute well for the whole team to be successful and get anywhere.

Clarifying and Appreciating Team Roles

Once your roles are pretty well established, you can also remind people of how they can best contribute to your team. When I first began my consulting career, I worked with the Arizona men's basketball team. They had a team of highly talented players who were all used to being the "Go to Guy" on their high school and AAU teams. However, with all the NBA-caliber talent at Arizona at every position, not everyone would be able to play major minutes.

To help the guys better understand and appreciate everyone's particular role, I had the players sit in a circle in the locker room. Rather than going around and having each guy talk about what he thought his role was on the team, I switched things up a bit. I asked the teammates of each player to talk about the two or three things the team needed the most from that particular player if the whole team was going to be successful and win a national championship. Some guys were obviously told they needed to consistently score in double digits for the team to win. Other guys were told they needed to grab 10 or more rebounds a game. Another player was told he needed to take pride in his defense and consistently shut down the other team's top scorer.

When it came to the reserve guys, they too were told how they could best contribute to the entire team's success. Some were challenged to go hard every single day in practice so they could push the starters and help the whole team get better. Many of the young guys were told they needed to be patient and keep a good attitude because they too would eventually get their chance to shine, either if an injury occurred, or in subsequent years as they matured and improved their games. Another guy was told his primary job was to bring energy to the team and keep everyone up and enthusiastic despite the long season. By the end, each player was reminded by his teammates specifically how he could best contribute to the team winning a national championship. And each player was reminded how important and valued his role was by the rest of his teammates, no matter how large or small it might have seemed from the outside.

Know, Accept, and Own Your Responsibilities and Role

Being an Accountable Teammate starts with knowing, accepting, and owning your roles and responsibilities. Invest the time to clarify exactly what is expected of you so you can step up and make the important contributions your team needs you to make.

CHAPTER 1
. . . .
EXTRA CREDIT ENRICHMENT EXERCISES

1. Clarify and Appreciate Your Team's Roles

After consulting with your coach to see if the timing is appropriate, you too could do a similar exercise as Arizona men's basketball did to help clarify and appreciate the roles on your team. Let each player know the primary things you expect and need from them for your whole team to be successful. These are the main things that you will expect from them and hold them accountable for bringing to your team.

2. Appreciate the Tough, Thankless, "Lug Nut" Jobs

As an Accountable Teammate, invest the time to acknowledge and appreciate the often obscure, thankless, yet essential "Lug Nut" type roles on your team. These "Lug Nuts" often don't get the praise and attention of those in more prominent roles, yet they are still essential for your team's success. Invest the time to identify the often overlooked and underappreciated roles on your team and let them know how much you value them and appreciate them. You might even present them with an actual Lug Nut and mention how critical they are for keeping your team rolling along, but realize they may be often taken for granted. This Lug Nut kind of appreciation can extend to your coaching staff and support staff as well. There are many people like athletic trainers, strength coaches, academic advisors, administrative assistants, guidance counselors, custodians, groundskeepers, athletic administrators, etc., who do super valuable things behind the scenes that are an important part of your team's success. Be sure to show them some Lug Nut love as well—it will make their day!

Which three "Lug Nut" people will you recognize and appreciate this week?

_____

_____

_____

3. Switch Roles for a Day

To further help people understand and appreciate each other's roles, talk with your coach to see if you can set up a practice where you switch roles for a few drills or an entire day, obviously making sure no one gets hurt. If you are football team, have your lineman try kicking field goals, your linebackers trying to complete passes to your kickers, etc. If you are a baseball team, have your pitchers and catchers trade places and your infielders become your outfielders. If you are a swimmer, swim a different one of your teammate's events. Trying to play another teammates' role you are less familiar with and skilled at is a great way for everyone to understand and appreciate the difficulties of everyone's roles and the challenges of doing their jobs.

TEAM MEETING NOTES

What are your Top 3-5 Biggest Takeaways and Action Items from this chapter?

1. _____
_____
_____

2. _____
_____
_____

3. _____
_____
_____

4. _____
_____
_____

5. _____
_____
_____

Which three people on your team do the best job of Owning their Responsibilities and Role? Why?

1. _____
_____
_____

2. _____
_____
_____

3. _____
_____
_____

Next Meeting Date:_____Time: _____

ACCOUNTABILITY PARTNER WEEKLY FEEDBACK SHEET—MODULE 2

Accountability Partner Name: _____

Date: _____

What exactly is expected/needed of you and how can you best contribute to the team this week?

WEEK 1

My Responsibility/Role/ Expectation/ Job this Week:	Impacts Whom?	Positive/Negative Consequences	Due Date?	Results Delivered?
				Yes or No
				Yes or No
				Yes or No
				Yes or No
				Yes or No
				Yes or No

AP Challenge: _____

(Which task can you put a fun/measurable consequence on with your AP if you deliver results?)

At the end of the week, have your Accountability Partner rate you on how accountable you were:

1. How well did he/she own and execute his/her responsibilities and role this week?

    1   2   3   4   5   6   7   8   9   10

2. How well did he/she recognize and respect his/her Ripple Effect?

    1   2   3   4   5   6   7   8   9   10

3. How well did he/she consider the consequences on others before acting?

    1   2   3   4   5   6   7   8   9   10

4. How well did he/she eliminate excuses?

    1   2   3   4   5   6   7   8   9   10

5. How well did he/she have your back as your Accountability Partner?

    1   2   3   4   5   6   7   8   9   10

6. How will did he/she keep his/her commitments and deliver results?

    1   2   3   4   5   6   7   8   9   10

Comments:

_____

_____

_____

_____

CHAPTER 2
RECOGNIZE YOUR RIPPLE EFFECT

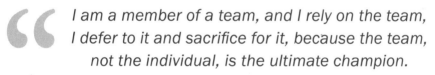

> *I am a member of a team, and I rely on the team,*
> *I defer to it and sacrifice for it, because the team,*
> *not the individual, is the ultimate champion.*

Mia Hamm, Soccer Superstar

When you choose to be a part of a team, it can no longer be just about you. You now have teammates and coaches who depend, rely, and count on you each and every day. They expect you to prioritize and fully commit to the team's mission over yourself. (Mission > Team > Teammate > Self) You must now realize that every one of your actions and attitudes impact numerous others, way beyond yourself. Your thoughts, feelings, actions, and inaction generate either a positive or negative Ripple Effect on many others. So, as an Accountable Teammate, it is absolutely critical that you fully understand both the subtle and significant impact you have on others and no longer cluelessly and selfishly think about, focus on, and worry just about yourself.

IT'S NOT ALL ABOUT YOU

San Antonio Spurs coach Gregg Popovich, when asked what he looks for when adding or drafting players to the team, said, "We're looking for people who have gotten over themselves. You can tell that pretty quick. You can talk to someone for four or five minutes and you can tell if it's about them, or if they understand they're just a piece of the puzzle. We look for that."

To be an Accountable Teammate you must realize and respect the fact that it is not all about you. It is not all about your stats, your playing time, your role, your moods, your feelings, your whatever. These things are understandably important to you but you must think beyond yourself and put them in context of the entire team. It can no longer solely be about what's best for you and your personal agenda—it must be about what is best for the TEAM. It must be about TEAM success and not individual success. (WE > me) You must expand your viewpoint of situations to encompass not just your solitary, often selfish viewpoint but to see things from a variety of perspectives, especially that of your teammates; to put yourself in other people's shoes and be aware of how things impact, benefit, frustrate, or hurt them from their unique and valuable vantage point and position on the team.

> "It's not about any one person. You've got to get over yourself and realize that it takes a group to get this thing done."

Gregg Popovich, San Antonio Spurs Coach

TO WHOM ARE YOU ACCOUNTABLE?

As an Accountable Teammate, you must remember that you are no longer an isolated individual but one who is closely interconnected and intertwined with your team and coaches and many others. What you do affects multitudes and similarly what others do influences you. Even if you are an athlete who plays an individual sport, your actions and attitudes still impact others even though you may not be interacting with them during the actual competition itself. Take a moment to list all the people your actions impact and to whom you are ultimately accountable.

Who are all the people that your attitudes and actions now directly impact or indirectly affect in some way, shape, or form?

_____

_____

_____

YOU'RE PART OF SOMETHING SO MUCH BIGGER THAN YOURSELF

Whether or not you realize it, your actions, choices, and decisions impact at least hundreds if not thousands of people. Don't believe me? As you'll see in the upcoming diagram, these people include your teammates, coaches, support staff, athletic administrators, classmates, past athletes, alumni, fans, kids in the community, etc. Every time you put on your uniform you represent these people.

Depending on the size of your team, school, community, alumni, fans, and how much media coverage your sport gets, you impact at least 100 to several million people on a regular basis. Most athletes may not even realize the vast numbers of people across campus and even around the world who are affected in some way by their actions.

> "When you are in public, in class, or when you post on social media, you represent ALL Spartans."

Dane Fife, Michigan State Men's Basketball Assistant Coach

STANDING ON THE SHOULDERS OF OTHERS

Some college coaches will have their current athletes research all the people who have worn their jersey number before them. They encourage their athletes to reach out to these people to get to know them and learn about what their experience was like when they were on the team. Obviously there is also a special bond when you share a jersey number with someone and hopefully you understand you are playing for them as well as yourself. Some coaches will even list the names of all the people who have worn that jersey before on the current athletes' lockers.

Having this appreciation for the history of the program provides you and your teammates with a better context, perspective, and understanding that numerous people put in a lot of time and effort to build the program before they even got there. As the Chinese Proverb says, "Those who drink the water must remember those who dug the well." Your program's past players have invested a great deal in you and your team's success. They too have poured their own blood, sweat, and tears into the program and want what is best for it. You now carry the baton and get to carry on that legacy.

Knowing that you are standing on the shoulders of others helps remind you that the locker room you change in, the field/court you play on, and the gear you have would likely not be possible without those who came before you. You reap the benefits of their hard work, their sacrifice, their accountability; and you also need to realize that your investment will in turn help athletes of future generations. So not only are you connected and accountable to your current teammates and coaches, but your past alumni, and even future people who will represent your team and wear the uniform. What you do is so powerful it actually impacts the past, present, and future.

BIG AND LITTLE EYES UPON YOU

Further, even your team's alumni from your school and fans from the community (and around the country) support your success, especially the young kids who look up to you. In their eyes, you are a hero. They admire you, watch your every move in good times and bad, and seek to emulate you. So you are also accountable to them as they too are highly invested in you and your team's success. The Little Eyes Upon You poem by Edgar Guest reminds you of that:

LITTLE EYES UPON YOU

*There are little eyes upon you
and they're watching night and day.*

*There are little ears that quickly
take in every word you say.*

*There are little hands all eager
to do anything you do;*

*And a little boy who's dreaming
of the day he'll be like you.*

*You're the little fellow's idol,
you're the wisest of the wise.*

*In his little mind about you
no suspicions ever rise.*

*He believes in you devoutly,
holds all you say and do;*

He will say and do, in your way
when he's grown up just like you.

There's a wide-eyed little fellow
who believes you're always right;
and his eyes are always opened,
and he watches day and night.
You are setting an example
every day in all you do;

For the little boy who's waiting
to grow up to be just like you.

POND ANALOGY

Hopefully you are beginning to fully comprehend the significant Ripple Effect you have on so many others far beyond just yourself. Much like tossing a rock into a pond, your actions and attitudes create a ripple effect across your team impacting them in large and small ways. Further, your Ripple Effect spreads out to a range far greater than you often realize and affects a multitude of people. And, just like if you were to toss a large boulder into a pond it would create a big splash, displace a lot of water, and send a huge wave throughout the rest of the pond, so too do some of your actions create a significant impact on others. Is that impact positive or negative?

TO WHOM DO YOU FEEL MOST CONNECTED AND ACCOUNTABLE?

Who specifically do you feel the most connected and accountable to? Use the Ripple Effect diagram on the next page to list the specific names of people to whom you feel the most accountable. For each of these groups (other than Future Teammates), write the names of the people who you feel the most connected to in the rings. You can then share the names with your Accountability Partner (and with your whole team in your weekly meeting if you are so moved). These are the people who support you through thick and thin and you never want to let down or disappoint.

As an Accountable Teammate, what you do influences and impacts others. You are not a solitary figure operating alone in a vacuum—but an interconnected energy force that both influences and is influenced by numerous others around you. You can use the tremendous power of this energy for good or for evil. Fortunately, you get to decide what kind of impact you want to have on your team.

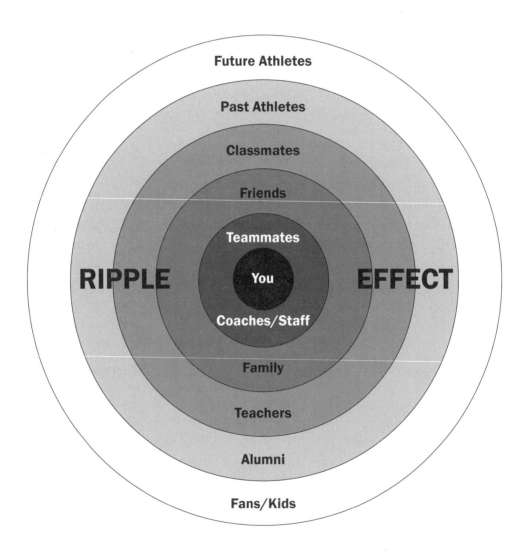

RESPECTING YOUR CONNECTIONS

Being accountable means not only being aware of your interconnections with other people but also being responsible for them and respectful to those you affect.

POWER TO INFLUENCE AND INSPIRE

Through your choices, decisions, attitudes, actions, and inaction, you have the amazing power to either positively or negatively influence and impact other people's lives. You have the ability to make your culture one that is positive and productive or one that is negative and destructive. You can either help set your teammates up for success or sabotage them for failure. Your attitudes and actions can either suck the life out of your teammates, coaches, and fans or inspire them to greatness.

For example, in response to the terrible Houston flooding from Hurricane Harvey, Houston Texans player J.J. Watt inspired people to donate to help flood victims. His original goal of $500,000 transformed into $32,000,000 because people were so inspired by J.J. to help.

Illinois swimmer CeCe Marizu and Central Michigan soccer player Amanda Waugh raised over $20,000 to build schools in Kenya to help children living in impoverished areas get an education.

Your WORDS ripple out to others and positively or negatively impact them.

Your ACTIONS ripple out to others and positively or negatively impact them.

Your REACTIONS to situations ripple out to others and positively or negatively impact them.

Your BODY LANGUAGE ripples out to others and positively or negatively impacts them.

Using our pond analogy, how specifically can the positive ripples you send out help calm the turbulent waters for your teammates and coaches to offer smooth sailing for them?

Or do the negative ripples you send out cause a tsunami for your teammates and coaches that rock their boats, cause them to fall overboard, and drown in your dysfunction?

How Can I Best Help, Contribute, Serve?

Part of being an Accountable Teammate is continually thinking about how you can help a fellow teammate. Consider what you can do today to set up a teammate for success, lighten their load, save them some valuable time, or make their day in some way. Text them an inspiring quote, bring them their water bottle, carry their gear, remind them how much you appreciate them, stay extra with them to work on their game. It doesn't have to be big, just helpful in some way. Of course don't do this because you feel you have to—do this because you genuinely want to; because you care about and respect your teammates so much that you want to help them in whatever way you can. When everyone in your program regularly thinks of ways to help and serve their teammates you create a very positive and productive culture on your team.

> Make Your AP's Day Today! How can you make things easier for your teammates and coaches? What can you do today that will help/contribute/serve your AP or another teammate? DO IT!!!

_____

_____

_____

Respect Your Ripple Effect and the Role Everyone Plays on Your Team

When you are part of a team, you must commit to treating others with respect, no matter what their role on your team might be. This means starters respecting reserves, seniors respecting freshmen, athletes respecting coaches—and vice versa. Each person on your team deserves your respect because you all should be pulling in the same direction and working hard toward the same goals. No one is above anyone else. You are not always going to like your teammates and their decisions all the time, but you must make a pact to treat them with respect.

Who Packs Your Parachute?

A great story about the importance of respecting everyone and the valuable role they play on your team comes from Captain Charlie Plumb, a decorated Navy fighter pilot during the Vietnam War. After flying 75 successful combat missions, Captain Plumb was shot down by the enemy and captured. He spent six years as a prisoner of war but was eventually released and won numerous awards for his valiant service to his country.

Several years later, Captain Plumb was eating in a restaurant with his wife when a man neither of them knew or had ever seen before excitedly approached.

"You're Captain Plumb!" the man said. "You flew jet fighters in Vietnam from the aircraft carrier Kitty Hawk. You were shot down!"

"How in the world did you know that?" asked Captain Plumb.

"I packed your parachute," the man replied. Captain Plumb gasped in surprise and gratitude. The man shook his hand and said, "I guess it worked!"

Captain Plumb assured him, "It sure did—if your 'chute hadn't worked, I wouldn't be here today."

Captain Plumb couldn't sleep that night because he kept thinking about the man at the restaurant—a man who admittedly he once couldn't have cared less for but who was busy toiling away in the bowels of the ship carefully packing his parachute because he was so committed to serve and save lives. Captain Plumb thought, "I wondered how many times I might have passed him on the ship. I wondered how many times I might have seen him and not even said good morning, how are you, or anything because, you see, I was a fighter pilot and he was just a sailor."

Captain Plumb was so caught up in himself and his ego as a revered fighter pilot that he didn't realize or respect all the people who helped him be successful. He didn't know any of the mechanics who worked on his plane to keep it operating in peak condition. He didn't know any of the air traffic controllers who warned him of approaching enemy aircraft. He didn't know any of the flight deck guys who kept him safe on the runway of the aircraft carrier. And regrettably, he didn't even know the man who packed his own parachute that ultimately saved his life, until the man came up to him many years later. When he speaks to people, Captain Plumb now challenges people with the critical question: *"Who packs your parachute?"*

APPLYING THE GOLDEN RULE

Ultimately, because you are so interconnected with your team, you must respect everyone and abide by the Golden Rule of doing unto your teammates as you would want them to do unto you. Treat others the way you would want to be treated. It doesn't matter what their position on the team might be, how old they are, or whether they start or rarely play. All deserve your recognition and respect as teammates because all contribute in some way to your common cause.

CHAPTER 2
. . . .
EXTRA CREDIT ENRICHMENT EXERCISES

1. Consider the people who pack your parachute. Who are the people who your success (and sometimes safety) depends on them doing their job? How well do you know/ appreciate them?

_____

_____

Whose parachute do you pack on your team? Who depends on you to do your job well?

_____

_____

How do they benefit if you do it well—or suffer if you do it poorly or not at all?

_____

_____

2. Research the past people who have worn your jersey number. Reach out to them to learn what things were like when they were on the team. Let them know how you will honor the number.

3. Discover who was instrumental in developing your facilities and locker room. Reach out to them to find out how your facilities came to be and what inspired them to create them. Let them know that you appreciate the chance to compete on and get ready in something they created.

4. Create a Ripple Effect Poster for your entire team. Talk with your teammates to get the names and ideally pictures of all the specific people they feel most connected and accountable to (friends, family, teachers, fans, alums, etc.). Put their names and/or faces on a Ripple Effect Poster and post it in your locker room as a continual reminder of all the people who you care about, who care about you, and who you play for. Dedicate your season to them.

5. UW-Milwaukee women's basketball coach Kyle Rechlicz has created Thank You for Packing My Parachute Cards. Each captain gets 10 cards a week and gives them out to people who positively impact their program. They then discuss as a team who received the cards and why.

TEAM MEETING NOTES

· ·

What are your Top 3-5 Biggest Takeaways and Action Items from this chapter?

1. _____
_____
_____

2. _____
_____
_____

3. _____
_____
_____

4. _____
_____
_____

5. _____
_____
_____

Which three people on your team do the best job of Recognizing Their Ripple Effect? Why?

1. _____
_____
_____

2. _____
_____
_____

3. _____
_____
_____

Next Meeting Date:_____Time: _____

ACCOUNTABILITY PARTNER WEEKLY FEEDBACK SHEET—MODULE 3

Accountability Partner Name: _____

Date: _____

What exactly is expected/needed of you and how can you best contribute to the team this week?

My Responsibility/Role/ Expectation/ Job this Week:	Impacts Whom?	Positive/Negative Consequences	Due Date?	Results Delivered?
				Yes or No
				Yes or No
				Yes or No
				Yes or No
				Yes or No
				Yes or No

WEEK 2

AP Challenge: _____

(Which task can you put a fun/measurable consequence on with your AP if you deliver results?)

At the end of the week, have your Accountability Partner rate you on how accountable you were:

1. How well did he/she own and execute his/her responsibilities and role this week?

    1   2   3   4   5   6   7   8   9   10

2. How well did he/she recognize and respect his/her Ripple Effect?

    1   2   3   4   5   6   7   8   9   10

3. How well did he/she consider the consequences on others before acting?

    1   2   3   4   5   6   7   8   9   10

4. How well did he/she eliminate excuses?

    1   2   3   4   5   6   7   8   9   10

5. How well did he/she have your back as your Accountability Partner?

    1   2   3   4   5   6   7   8   9   10

6. How will did he/she keep his/her commitments and deliver results?

    1   2   3   4   5   6   7   8   9   10

Comments:

_____

_____

_____

_____

CHAPTER 3

CONSIDER THE CONSEQUENCES

*When considering the consequences
of not doing the little things, you realize
there are no little things.*

Brad Stevens, Boston Celtics Coach

Because your success and failure is closely intertwined with that of your teammates, as an Accountable Athlete you always must invest the time to consider how your words, behaviors, actions, reactions, energy levels, and even body language might affect your teammates. Much like a series of dominoes, your choices create a chain reaction that influences other events. You must get in the consistent habit of thinking before speaking and acting. You must consciously consider how your every action, interaction, and even inaction could impact your team.

3 CRITICAL QUESTIONS TO CONSIDER BEFORE YOU ACT

Especially if you are about to do something that you are uncertain about, have an uneasy feeling about, or are worried about in some way, stop and consider these critical questions:

1. How could this impact my teammates and/or coaches?

2. How could this impact our team's chances of success?

3. How could this impact our team's reputation?

As an Accountable Teammate, you must consider all the possible and likely answers to these important questions before you act. Here are some unfortunate examples of athletes who didn't fully consider the consequences before they acted:

Pittsburgh Steelers receiver Antonio Brown secretly posted his coach's postgame talk live on social media, without the coach knowing or getting his permission. In the talk, Mike Tomlin, the Steelers coach, mentioned some unkind things about their upcoming opponents, the New England Patriots, for the whole world to hear. Of course the Patriots saw the video, which only provided them with some extra motivation to beat the Steelers the following week 36-17 on the way to winning the Super Bowl.

Harvard men's soccer created a written rating system of the physical appearance of the female student-athletes at the school. When the highly inappropriate document was discovered by administrators midway through the year, the rest of their season was cancelled.

Tennis player Maria Sharapova took a banned substance and was suspended for two years from playing tennis. She lost millions of dollars in endorsement deals with American Express, Tag Heuer, and Avon.

There are obviously numerous others we could list but you get the picture. The point is: Accountable Athletes consciously and carefully consider the consequences BEFORE they act so they can minimize or eliminate the chances of hurting themselves, their team, and others.

YOUR WHOLE TEAM IS HELPED OR HURT BY YOUR CHOICES

One of the primary reasons why some coaches hold the whole team accountable for one person's mistake is that a single person's choices and actions can have serious consequences that impact everyone on your team. *One person's choices can be the margin between winning and losing.*

- If one athlete turns over the ball, your whole team loses possession.

- If one person misses a coach's base-running sign, your whole team is thrown out at home plate.

- If one person doesn't guard/mark their person, your whole team gets scored on.

- If one player commits an unsportsmanlike act in football, the whole team is penalized 15 yards.

- If one person gets arrested for driving under the influence, your whole team's reputation suffers.

- If one athlete cheats on a test, the whole school thinks your team is a bunch of cheaters.

- If one player lacks focus and attention to detail, your whole team pays the price of losing.

The physical, mental, tactical, and personal mistakes and breakdowns of a single person impact your whole team. Your sloppiness, tardiness, and selfishness hurts your teammates and coaches. It makes their life tougher, it doubles their work, it sets them back, it gives them a black eye, it keeps them from winning championships. Everyone on your team is impacted by your actions—just as you are theirs. Your problems become our problems. Keep in mind that:

- When you quit on yourself, you also quit on your teammates and coaches.

- When you embarrass yourself, you also embarrass your teammates and coaches.

- When you let down yourself, you also let down your teammates and coaches.

- When you push yourself, you also push your teammates and coaches.

- When you inspire yourself, you also inspire your teammates and coaches.

- When you lead yourself, you also lead your teammates and coaches.

Because your choices have consequences that impact so many others, you must think through the consequences of your words and actions before you say them and before you do them. You must ask yourself, "Is this what I want to do to my teammates? Is this what I want to do to my brothers/sisters? Is this what I want to do to my coaches? Do I want to help them or hurt them?"

"A good teammate thinks before he acts. A good teammate knows
to think before he speaks; words have meaning and it can't be
about one person, it's about team."

Buck Showalter, Major League Baseball Manager

INDIVIDUAL DISCIPLINE OR TEAM DISCIPLINE?

That is exactly why rather than having one person be disciplined and run for being late, the whole team is often held accountable and disciplined for it, either through extra conditioning or some other unpleasant yet instructive means. This kind of collective team discipline for an individual's careless or selfish error penalizes the whole team and is the hallmark of a Culture of Accountability. It emphasizes the point that your whole team is indeed interconnected, that teammate's actions have powerful Ripple Effects far beyond themselves, and that people must consider the consequences on the whole team rather than just themselves before they act selfishlessly and/or inappropriately and get the whole team in trouble.

If your whole team is punished and runs when one person is late, you can bet that you, or at least someone on your team, will let the offending teammate know how important the team standard of being on time is and they better quickly get their stuff together. Your team leaders will ideally talk with the offender and remind them of their responsibilities to the team and how not living up to them hurts everyone. And you and your teammates will exert a strong amount of peer pressure on them to be more responsible because you don't want to have to run again. Finally, you will also likely hold them accountable and check up on them before the next practice to ensure that they are on time. You now claim accountability for making sure both you and they are on time—because if you don't, you know that you and your whole team will suffer: just as you will if they let you down on the court, field, track, course, etc. You hold them accountable to do the right thing, help your team, pull their weight, do their job, and contribute the way you need them to.

"On good teams coaches hold players accountable,
on great teams players hold players accountable."

Joe Dumars, NBA Champion

YOUR 3 POINT ACCOUNTABILITY TEST

How do you know whether or not you should be held accountable for something—or if you should hold a teammate or coach accountable for something? You can use this 3 Point Accountability Test for virtually any situation you might face to determine whether or not you should and will be held accountable for it:

1. Did you cause it?

2. Did you contribute to it?

3. Did you condone it?

If you answer "yes" to any of these three questions, you will be held accountable to some degree for it, especially if you are looked to or have the title of a team leader. Let's break down each of these questions so you and your teammates clearly understand what each one means because they are slightly yet significantly different.

Did you cause it?

Obviously if you are the primary cause of something you should be held accountable for it. For example, if you consume a large amount of alcohol, get into a car and drive impaired, and cause an accident, you will be held accountable for it. Any action or inaction you take that directly or primarily causes something to happen you can and should be fully accountable for.

Did you contribute to it?

The next question to explore in determining whether or not you are accountable for something is: Did you in some reasonable way contribute to it? While you may not be the direct cause of some situations, your action or inaction indirectly allowed it to happen or played a reasonable role for it to occur. In short, you in some way contributed to the situation even though you might not have directly caused it. Let's say the driver in the first example was under 21 but you were the person who purchased and gave them the alcohol. While you didn't get into the car and cause the accident, your action of buying or providing the alcohol for an under-aged person certainly contributed to the DUI accident happening, even though it was indirectly.

Did you condone it?

Finally, the last question you need to consider is: Did you condone it? Condoning the behavior means that you saw or sensed something was a potential problem or clearly wrong but rather than intervening and doing something about it, you

IF YOU CAUSE IT, CONTRIBUTE TO IT, OR CONDONE IT, YOU ARE ACCOUNTABLE FOR IT.

said nothing and allowed it to occur. Staying with our DUI example, condoning the situation means that you saw the drunk person grabbing their keys and walking to their car, knowing full well they have had too much to drink and should not be driving because they were a serious risk of hurting themselves and others, and you said and did nothing. While you did not provide the person with the alcohol nor hand them their keys, help them into their car, and encourage them to drive home, you still witnessed a likely problematic situation and chose to ignore it rather than try to change it. In essence, your inaction was a conscious choice not to get involved and potentially stop the dangerous situation—thereby condoning it.

> "The only thing necessary for the triumph of evil is
> for good men to do nothing."

Edmund Burke, British Statesman

Unfortunately, let's play this situation out to its potential conclusion and say that the drunk driver got into a terrible accident that not only killed themselves but also killed an innocent family of four who tragically happened to be in the wrong place at the wrong time. Who would you hold accountable for this situation in any way and how much are each of them responsible based on their actions or inaction?

How accountable is the Drunk Driver? Why or why not?

_____

_____

_____

How accountable is the Alcohol Provider? Why or why not?

_____

_____

_____

How accountable are the Bystanders? Why or why not?

_____

_____

_____

WEEK
3

Certainly the drunk driver would be primarily responsible and accountable because their extremely poor choices directly led to the accident. So too would the person who provided the alcohol to the under-aged person be considered legally and morally accountable to contributing to this tragedy. And finally the bystanders, who witnessed the clearly drunk person get into the car and drive away, would also likely feel a tremendous sense of guilt and remorse for having condoned the situation that killed the driver and the family of four. In this example, all were accountable in some way and could have prevented the tragedy in some way either by changing their actions that caused, contributed to, or condoned the situation. If you would feel even a slight twinge of guilt or remorse if something went wrong with whatever situation you are facing, there is a good chance that you would be in some way accountable for it.

While most of the situations you will be involved in will not be as serious and life-threatening as a drunk driver, ultimately, you too will be held accountable by your coaches and teammates for the situations you cause, contribute to, and condone. These apply to potentially problematic situations like a teammate:

- skips their offseason workouts

- misses classes

- hazes your newcomers

- trashes the coaching staff in the locker room

- drinks on the bus or in the hotel at away games

- cheats on tests and exams

- smokes marijuana on the weekends

If you are doing these things, encouraging these behaviors, or aware of these behaviors but doing nothing to stop or curb them, you too will be held accountable for them because they all negatively impact your team. Keep in mind that most coaches and athletic administrators will hold you accountable for the problematic actions of your teammates, especially if you are a team captain or core team leader.

4 LEVELS OF TEAM DISCIPLINE

In a Culture of Accountability, you will see four levels of discipline in place to ensure that people complete their responsibilities and are accountable to each other.

Level 1 Discipline—Personal Responsibility

The first level of discipline is based on Personal Responsibility. As covered in *The Athlete's Responsibility Manual,* Personal Responsibility means you do what is expected of you, fulfill your duties, and follow your team's rules because you personally believe in them. You show up on time, work hard in practice, complete the weight workouts, eat well, train in the offseason, etc.,

4 LEVELS OF TEAM DISCIPLINE

4 LEVELS OF TEAM DISCIPLINE
Level 1 — Personal Responsibility
Level 2 — Team Accountability
Level 3 — Captains Confront
Level 4 — Coach Confronts

because you know these things are important to your success. You basically do what needs to be done because you want to; you see the sheer value in it and you responsibly and willingly do it. You take personal responsibility for your training because it is the right thing to do.

WEEK **3**

> How well does your team currently have Level 1 Discipline in place on a 1 to 10 scale?
>
> 1   2   3   4   5   6   7   8   9   10
>
> If you did not rate your team at least a 9 or 10, what specifically can you do to improve it?
>
> _____
>
> _____
>
> _____

Level 2 Discipline—Team Accountability

The second level of Team Discipline is based on Team Accountability. Your motivation now to abide by your team's expectations, standards, and rules is primarily based on being fully accountable to your teammates. You feel you owe it to them to do the right thing and help the team. You do it not just for yourself but you also do it for your teammates. You are able to get out of yourself and into your team. As we said in the previous chapter, you Realize the Ripple Effect you have on your teammates and know that your actions create positive or negative consequences for them. Now you do things not just for yourself but also so you can contribute to your team's success because you know you are answerable to them. Athletes who abide by Level 2 Discipline would never want to let down their teammates or hurt them in any way.

How well does your team currently have Level 2 Discipline in place on a 1 to 10 scale?

1   2   3   4   5   6   7   8   9   10

If you did not rate your team at least a 9 or 10, what specifically can you do to improve it?

_____

_____

_____

Level 3 Discipline—Captains Confront

A third level of Discipline ideally kicks in with your team when your team leaders hold people accountable to your team's expectations, standards, and rules. This level needs to occur when you have teammates who don't take personal responsibility for themselves and/or they don't understand or value their connection and accountability to their teammates. They seem to have their own agenda, are clueless or couldn't care less about their negative impact on the team, and your captains must clarify your team's expectations for their behavior and set them straight. The problem with Level 3 Discipline is that many team captains are ill-equipped, reluctant, or outright scared to play this necessary Enforcer role. They fail to hold people accountable to your team's expectations, which frustrates the rest of the team and kills the captain's credibility. When Level 3 Discipline from the team captains is weak or non-existent, your last hope to preserve a Culture of Accountability is with your coaches at Level 4.

"The entire aim of our policies at Tennessee is to get our athletes to discipline each other. . . .We have evolved a system in which I don't have to do a whole lot of punishing, penalizing, or pushing them. Our upperclassmen become the disciplinarians of our team instead of me."

Pat Summitt, Legendary Tennessee Women's Basketball Coach

How well does your team currently have Level 3 Discipline in place on a 1 to 10 scale?

1   2   3   4   5   6   7   8   9   10

If you did not rate your team at least a 9 or 10, what specifically can you do to improve it?

_____

_____

_____

Level 4 Discipline—Coach Confronts

Finally, the last line of defense for discipline on your team is when your coach confronts your teammates who are not accountable. When it gets down to Level 4 Discipline it is obviously more serious. If someone doesn't abide by your team's expectations and rules because they aren't personally responsible enough to do so, they don't care about their connection to their teammates and how it adversely affects them, and they won't listen to or respect your team leaders who have confronted them about their concerning or detrimental behavior, it is time to bring in the big guns—your coach. Being in a position of ultimate authority, your coach should ideally have the clout, maturity, respect, and leadership skills to effectively discipline the person. They should be able to have a serious discussion with the person about their serious behavior, what needs to be quickly and permanently corrected, and the consequences for doing so or not doing so. Ultimately, if your coach doesn't hold people accountable and preserve your team's Culture of Accountability, all the other Levels of Discipline will soon erode and crumble within your team. So just as it is critical for you to hold yourself accountable, it is also essential for your coach to hold you and your teammates accountable to your team's expectations and standards.

WEEK
3

How well does your team currently have Level 4 Discipline in place on a 1 to 10 scale?

1   2   3   4   5   6   7   8   9   10

If you did not rate your team at least a 9 or 10, what would you suggest your coach could do to improve it?

_____

_____

_____

CONSEQUENCES

Finally, not only should people be clear about the expectations your team has for them and their role, but also clear about the consequences when they meet, exceed, and fall below your team's standards.

Positive Consequences for Meeting and Exceeding Expectations

Ideally your team has a positive incentive structure in place when your teammates meet and especially exceed your team's expectations. Holding people accountable is not just about penalizing them when they do wrong but also praising them when they do well. Be sure you positively call out your teammates, coaches, and support staff when they meet and exceed your expectations, successfully play their role, deliver results, contribute to the team, and masterfully do their jobs. Praising these positive actions not only acknowledges and appreciates them but it serves as an incentive for others to do their job well too.

Sincere praise and compliments go a long way to acknowledge your teammates and are the quickest, easiest, and often most meaningful way of valuing their contributions. Use them often as few people ever complain about feeling over-appreciated.

Working with your coach, you can also put some strategies in place to more formally acknowledge the people who make noteworthy contributions to you team, such as the honored athlete gets:

- Player of the Week Award

- Game Ball Award—Alabama Football gives a Ball Out Belt for creating turnovers

- Helmet Sticker

- Choice of the playlist for warmup, practice, and/or pregame

- First choice of seats on the van, bus, plane or where to go for the team meal

- Chance to plan a portion of or the entire practice

- Plus Points to get them out of running sprints

Find something that appropriately acknowledges those who meet and especially exceed your team's expectations to recognize and reward your teammates.

How well does your team acknowledge and appreciate those who meet and exceed expectations?

     1   2   3   4   5   6   7   8   9   10

What positive consequences does your team have for those who meet and exceed expectations?

_____

_____

_____

Negative Consequences for Falling Below Expectations

Conversely, unfortunately there will be times when teammates fall below your team's expectations, standards, and rules. Obviously if the person barely misses your expectations and tries with all their might you will approach them differently than if they are nowhere near your expectations and deliberately abuse them.

Teammates who try their best and just miss expectations need reminders, support, and your confidence in them that they can get there. Teammates who consistently or blatantly abuse your team's expectations need to be dealt with much more seriously. The goal of providing negative consequences is more to educate and enlighten them rather than punish them. You want them to see how their behavior hurt your team's chances of success or sullied your team's hard-earned reputation. In seeing how they hurt their teammates and made their lives tougher, it should motivate them to correct their actions so that they don't repeat the mistake in the future.

As we discussed before, holding the whole team accountable for an individual's mistake reminds everyone that your collective success and failure is highly interconnected. So many coaches will apply the negative consequences to the whole team rather than just to the offending individual.

Withholding privileges is another way to provide negative consequences to those who consciously and consistently fail to meet your team's expectations, standards, and rules. Being on your team is a privilege, representing your team is a privilege, wearing your jersey is a privilege, using your locker room is a privilege, and even practicing with your team is a privilege that you must earn and maintain. When you don't appreciate and abide by the important expectations of your teammates and coaches, you jeopardize your trust with them and may temporarily or permanently lose the privileges you earned as a respected member of the team. Effective ways to provide negative consequences to those who seriously and consistently fail to meet your team's expectations are to withhold privileges from them. This might mean not allowing them to practice with the team, not allowing them to use the locker room, or not allowing them to wear your team's gear for practices.

How well does your team hold accountable those who fail to meet expectations?

1   2   3   4   5   6   7   8   9   10

What negative consequences does your team have for those who fail to meet expectations?

_____

_____

_____

Just as you need to be clear about your responsibilities and roles, you also need to understand what will happen to you and your team when you meet them and when you don't.

CHAPTER 3
· ·
EXTRA CREDIT ENRICHMENT EXERCISES

1. Talk with an athlete from another team and ask them to rate how well they have the Four Levels of Team Discipline for their team. What can you learn from how they do discipline?

_____

_____

_____

_____

_____

2. Talk with an athlete from another team and ask them what positive consequences their team has to reward those who consistently meet and exceed their team's expectations and standards.

_____

_____

_____

_____

_____

3. Talk with an athlete from another team and ask them what negative consequences they have to educate (penalize) those who consistently fall below their team's expectations and standards.

_____

_____

_____

_____

_____

TEAM MEETING NOTES

What are your Top 3-5 Biggest Takeaways and Action Items from this chapter?

1. _____
_____
_____

2. _____
_____
_____

3. _____
_____
_____

4. _____
_____
_____

5. _____
_____
_____

Which three people on your team do the best job of Considering the Consequences? Why?

1. _____
_____
_____

2. _____
_____
_____

3. _____
_____
_____

Next Meeting Date:_____Time: _____

ACCOUNTABILITY PARTNER WEEKLY FEEDBACK SHEET—MODULE 4

Accountability Partner Name: _____

Date: _____

What exactly is expected/needed of you and how can you best contribute to the team this week?

My Responsibility/Role/ Expectation/ Job this Week:	Impacts Whom?	Positive/Negative Consequences	Due Date?	Results Delivered?
				Yes or No
				Yes or No
				Yes or No
				Yes or No
				Yes or No
				Yes or No

AP Challenge: _____

(Which task can you put a fun/measurable consequence on with your AP if you deliver results?)

At the end of the week, have your Accountability Partner rate you on how accountable you were:

1. How well did he/she own and execute his/her responsibilities and role this week?

    1   2   3   4   5   6   7   8   9   10

2. How well did he/she recognize and respect his/her Ripple Effect?

    1   2   3   4   5   6   7   8   9   10

3. How well did he/she consider the consequences on others before acting?

    1   2   3   4   5   6   7   8   9   10

4. How well did he/she eliminate excuses?

    1   2   3   4   5   6   7   8   9   10

5. How well did he/she have your back as your Accountability Partner?

    1   2   3   4   5   6   7   8   9   10

6. How will did he/she keep his/her commitments and deliver results?

    1   2   3   4   5   6   7   8   9   10

Comments:

_____

_____

_____

_____

WEEK
3

CHAPTER 4
ELIMINATE EXCUSES

" *He that is good for making excuses is seldom good for making anything else.* "

Benjamin Franklin

WEEK

4

Climbing Mount Kilimanjaro in Tanzania is an extraordinary accomplishment in its own right. Imagine accomplishing this amazing feat without any feet (or hands, forearms, or shins). Google Kyle Maynard. Born a quadruple amputee, Kyle didn't let that "excuse" stop him from becoming a championship wrestler, MMA fighter, and world-class mountaineer. With only stumps for arms and legs, Kyle bear-crawled 19,431 feet over 10 days to reach the snow-crested peak of Mount Kilimanjaro. If that wasn't enough, four years later he summited Argentina's Mount Aconcagua, the highest peak in both the Western and Southern hemispheres at 22,838 feet. Kyle's excellent book about his life and unimaginable accomplishments is appropriately titled, *No Excuses*.

Kyle says, "I've always believed that anyone can achieve their dreams, regardless. I've always had this attitude about no excuses; a belief that I can go on and do what I need to do. To go on, to succeed, regardless." He adds, "I don't give up on things. Every excuse that we make keeps us away from the things that we want most out of life." If Kyle doesn't use any excuses for climbing life's tallest mountains, you shouldn't either.

One of the best things you can do to be an Accountable Teammate is to make a pact with yourself and your teammates to Eliminate Excuses from your life. Eliminating Excuses means that you refuse to blame someone or something else for your situation. Eliminating Excuses means you won't point fingers at your teammates, coaches, equipment, officials, weather, etc. Eliminating Excuses means you will be fully accountable for everything you did and didn't do to cause or contribute to a certain result. This kind of complete accountability is critical to earning and maintaining the trust and respect of your teammates.

Those in the military especially know that a Culture of Excuses cannot be tolerated, especially when lives are on the line. One of the first things taught to brand new cadets at West Point is the importance of taking responsibility for their actions and being accountable to the team.

Author Ed Ruggerro writes about how new Army cadets at West Point are taught the importance of responsibility and accountability in the book *Duty First*. Instructors tell the cadets: "New cadet, you are allowed four responses: 'Yes, sir,' 'No, sir,' 'No excuse, sir,' and 'Sir, I do not understand.' New cadet, what are your four responses?" It takes a couple of tries before the neophytes learn the codes. It will take a little longer for them to stop trying to explain things. In that phrase, "No excuse, sir" (or "ma'am") is an early, critical lesson. Take responsibility for your actions. Always. No matter what the consequences."

So make a pact with your teammates and coaches that excuses will no longer be offered or tolerated for any mistakes, errors, failures or losses. You can and should seek valid reasons and explanations for why these negative situations occurred but never offer excuses for them.

WHAT'S THE DIFFERENCE BETWEEN EXPLANATIONS AND EXCUSES?

Failure is obviously a big part of both sports and life. You are going to make thousands of mistakes, lose dozens of games, and fail your share of tests. Everyone does. However, the key difference between winners and losers is how they either responsibly explain or irresponsibly try to excuse their role in the situation. Winners seek and provide legitimate explanations for failure and their role in it whereas losers search for and offer up lame excuses and try to put the blame on others. There is a subtle yet super significant difference between an explanation and excuse. The primary distinction is that an explanation focuses on owning the problem and taking 100% accountability for it whereas an excuse focuses on shifting accountability away from oneself and on to an external and often uncontrollable factor.

Explanation—An explanation provides a rational reason for why a mistake, failure, or loss occurred where the person giving it takes full responsibility and accountability for their role in why it happened. As an example, "The reason we lost this game is because my teammates and I didn't play solid defense. We made too many errors, didn't react well to what the other team threw at us, and allowed them to dictate the tempo." The person/team takes complete ownership for their role in situation.

Excuse—An excuse attempts to justify or explain away a mistake, failure, or loss by shifting the blame away from oneself and on to someone or something else. For example, "We lost the game because the officials were horrible, the weather was bad, and the other team cheated." The goal of the excuse is to protect and save oneself from accountability and dump it elsewhere.

> "You fail all the time, but you aren't a failure
> until you start blaming someone else."
>
> **Bum Phillips, NFL Coach**

The table below highlights the big differences between lame excuses and legit explanations:

EXCUSE vs.	EXPLANATION
Goal is self-preservation and saving face	Goal is to find and fix the problem
Person shifts responsibility for situation	Person states responsibility for situation
Person denies their accountability	Person declares their accountability
Person plays the Blame Game	Person plays the Claim Game
Person shades the truth	Person seeks the truth
Person fabricates falsehoods	Person finds facts
Person feels defensive to deflect problem	Person feels determined to discover problem

Person tries to justify their action/inaction	Person tries to correct their action/inaction
Person formulates an alibi	Person formulates an action plan
Excuse making kills credibility	*Explanation providing keeps credibility*
Excuse making erodes respect	*Explanation providing earns respect*
Excuse making destroys trust	*Explanation providing develops trust*
Team sees the person as devious	*Team sees the person as dependable*

As you can see, there is a significant difference between making lame excuses and providing legitimate explanations. Sure, there will be numerous times when officials make horrible calls, the weather is bad, and the other team plays unfairly, however you are still responsible and accountable for how you prepare for and handle these situations. While they definitely provide challenges, they are not insurmountable if you are fully accountable for what you can control and focus your attention and energies there. You know these obstacles are likely to happen so it is up to you to be accountable for them so that they don't distract, disrupt, or derail you and your teammates. Don't fall for the other team trying to get in your head. Don't put yourself in a position where you let an official or a bad bounce decide a game.

HOW TO BE ACCOUNTABLE BY ELIMINATING EXCUSES

There are two essential ways to Eliminate Excuses from your life—one you do on the front end before the problem occurs and the other you do on the back end after the mistake has happened:

1. Prepare for and Prevent Problems

2. Play the Claim Game Not the Blame Game

1. Prepare for and Prevent Problems

A great way to Eliminate Excuses is to plan for and prevent them on the front end. As Ben Franklin said, "An ounce of prevention is worth a pound of cure." Most people think accountability is something you do when things have already gone wrong. However the most effective kind of accountability is front-end accountability—preventing problems from even occurring in the first place. You can short-circuit the need for excuses by doing everything within your power to proactively avoid them through diligent and conscientious preparation.

For example, those who live in the Midwest and Northeast know there will be snowstorms in the winter. They don't freak out over them or use them as excuses for not getting to school or going to work. They expect them and prepare accordingly, even if they get several inches of snow. To stay warm in the frigid weather, they put on winter jackets, hats, gloves, and boots. To clear their driveways, sidewalks, and roads, they invest in shovels, snowblowers, snowplows, and road salt. They properly prepare ahead of time so that when a heavy snowstorm hits, the kind that debilitates and shuts down most other areas of the country for days on end, they don't let the adverse weather faze them or use it as an excuse.

You can prepare for and prevent potential problems in the same way to avoid excuses. Let's say you and your teammates need to be up super early for a workout or because you are traveling to a competition that is far away. Seeing that it is so early and many of your teammates love to sleep in, you know there is a decent chance someone might oversleep and they could be late or miss their ride. You can either hope you and your teammates get up on time or you can put in some sensible safeguards to ensure that everyone is where they are supposed to be when they are supposed to be there. Some things you could do to make sure everyone is accountable is to:

- Encourage everyone to set an alarm

- Encourage everyone to have a backup, second alarm set

- Coordinate with your Accountability Partner to text each other 45 minutes before the time to ensure you are both awake

- Set the expectation to arrive 15 minutes early as the standard—that way you have a little buffer time to work with

By consciously setting up these safeguards, buffers, and back up plans with your teammates, you dramatically minimize the chances that someone will be late for a workout or team meeting, miss a bus, van, or plane ride to an important competition, and let your teammates down.

Similarly, look at the typical excuses that people might offer in your sport. Then think of what you and your teammates can do to minimize and possibly eliminate this excuse.

- Sun was in my eyes

- Surface was slippery

- Didn't know the plays

- Coach put me in a new position

- Key athlete was injured

- Umpires, refs, officials, judges were bad

At least 50% of the excuses people attempt to use could be eliminated on the front end through better preparation, planning, and prevention. Make a commitment to yourself and your teammates that you will conscientiously and thoroughly prepare for potential problems *before they occur so you can minimize and prevent their negative effects as much as possible.*

What Could Go Wrong	Your Plan to Deal with It	Back Up Plan

2. Play the Claim Game Not the Blame Game

The other part of Eliminating Excuses occurs on the back end—after the problem, mishap, error, loss, failure, etc., has already occurred. Rather than searching for an excuse to pin the problem on someone else, Accountable Teammates accept full responsibility and accountability for it. They own it completely instead of trying to justify it. In effect, they play the Claim Game, own the situation and believe it happened or didn't happen because of their own actions or inaction.

> "You can find a thousand excuses in the game of football. Some of them might even be legitimate, but we don't want to hear them at Ohio State. You screw up, you own it, and then you work twice as hard to make sure it doesn't happen again."
>
> **Urban Meyer, Ohio State Football Coach**

WHEN YOU PLAY THE BLAME GAME EVERYONE LOSES

Playing the Blame Game means attempting to shift the responsibility for the problem away from yourself and on to someone or something else that is often outside of your control.

For example, I can remember being asked to work with a program that was really struggling. When I talked with the athletes of the team to figure out exactly what was going on, they complained the coaches weren't playing the right people, using the right strategy in games, or training and conditioning the team in the right way. The athletes thought the coaches were the primary problem and needed to change (or be changed) for the situation to get any better. When I asked the athletes how much of the team's problems were due to the coaching staff, they complained that 90% of the issues the team experienced was due to the coaches.

Of course the coaching staff had a drastically different viewpoint. They were highly frustrated by the team's lack of focus and effort in practices and the weight room, the athletes were not successfully executing the game plan, there was poor leadership in the locker room, and the athletes lacked the desire to work on their game. They too thought the only way to improve the situation was for the athletes to make significant changes or to recruit new ones. When I asked the coaches how much of the team's problems were due to their concerns with the athletes, the coaches estimated that 85% of problems were based on the athletes.

Unfortunately, both sides blamed the other and were not aware of or accountable for how they contributed to the problems. It was much easier to complain about what the other group was doing or not doing than it was to analyze, accept, and be accountable for their part in the problem. Obviously this situation was only getting worse because each group almost entirely blamed the other side for the frustrations rather than looking within and owning their part of the problem and coming up with solutions for it.

After hearing out the athletes and the coaches, we were able to get both sides to refocus on to the perceived 10-15% of the problem they thought they were personally responsible for. In doing so, it was remarkable how much progress was made when they stopped blaming the other side and started being more accountable for their "small" part of the problem and finding solutions for it.

Playing the Blame Game makes someone or something else the scapegoat for the problems. Instead of shouldering the load for your difficulties, you unfairly and unceremoniously dump them on others. While it provides you with a convenient way to try to absolve yourself from the issue, you place the crux of the problem on someone else. This approach obviously avoids the real issue, causes animosity with others, and only escalates and prolongs the problem.

PLAY THE CLAIM GAME NOT THE BLAME GAME

How do you and your teammates handle it when things go wrong? Who or what do you have a tendency to blame for mistakes, errors, losses, and losing seasons?

_____

_____

_____

Those who try to Play the Blame Game attempt to pass off the responsibility and accountability for their failure to someone or something else. Excuse makers seek sympathy rather than success.

BLAME GAME PLAYBOOK	CLAIM GAME PLAYBOOK
Complain	Responsibility
Blame	Accountability
Not My Job	Ownership
Denial	Truth
Cover Up	Transparency
Confusion	Clarity

THE 6 MOST POPULAR PLAYS IN THE BLAME GAME PLAYBOOK INCLUDE:

1. Complain

Unfortunately, the absolute easiest thing to do when there is a problem is to complain about it. Complaining is the default position for the Negative Nellie's on your team. They let everyone know that something is wrong and seem to derive a perverse sense of joy and pleasure in bemoaning and belaboring the problems. Rather than griping and moaning about problems and bringing down the rest of the team, Accountable Teammates assess the situation, enlist others' viewpoints, find the root cause of it, devise an intelligent plan to fix, and take action to solve the problem.

> "Losers assemble in small groups and complain.
> Winners assemble as a team and find ways to win."
>
> **Bill Parcells, NFL Coach**

WEEK
4

As you look at yourself, your Accountability Partner (AP), and your team, circle how often you complain about problems/struggles/losses rather than focus on solving them?

Self Rating:	Never	Seldom	Sometimes	Often	Always
AP Rating:	Never	Seldom	Sometimes	Often	Always
Team Rating:	Never	Seldom	Sometimes	Often	Always

2. Blame

Blaming someone or something else for your failure is the hallmark of the Blame Game. When problems occur, many athletes are quick to find fault with someone or something outside of themselves. Errors and mistakes are often blamed on things like adverse weather conditions, incompetent officiating, faulty equipment, poor playing conditions, etc. While blaming things for your failure is bad enough, it is even worse to blame the people on your own team. One of the quickest ways to lose your teammates' and coaches' trust and respect is to blame them for problems. If you try to blame the loss on your teammates because of their poor play or lack of effort, or your coaches because of inept strategy and play calling, I can guarantee you will have a frustrated team on your hands and damage your credibility, respect, and trust with them.

As you look at yourself, your Accountability Partner, and your team, how often do you blame someone or something else as the reason for your problems/struggles/losses?

Self Rating:	Never	Seldom	Sometimes	Often	Always
AP Rating:	Never	Seldom	Sometimes	Often	Always
Team Rating:	Never	Seldom	Sometimes	Often	Always

3. It's Not My Job

Thinking and acting as if a problem is "Not My Job" is another common strategy in the Blame Game Playbook. These people see the problem but because they perceive it as being outside of their position, role, or jurisdiction, they let it slide and wait for others to address it rather than doing what they can to help. As an example, this might be the teammate not holding another teammate accountable to the team's standards and expectations because they don't have the title of captain. Or the football punter thinking it is not his job to make a touchdown-saving tackle.

A great example of the "Not My Job" mentality is the cartoon of the boat sinking. While people on one of the end of the boat where the hole is try frantically to bail out the water flooding in, the guy on the other side of the boat just idly watches and calmly and cluelessly remarks, "I am glad the hole is not on my side of the boat."

Accountable Teammates realize: You're all in the same boat! You're all going to sink and possibly drown if the holes and leaks on your team don't get quickly noticed, bailed out, and successfully fixed—no matter what your role, position, or job might be. Rather than hoping and waiting for others to be aware of and address the issues, Accountable Teammates realize it is everyone's job to make sure the team is positively and productively rowing in the right direction without taking on water. Even though a situation may not be your primary role, you are still actively involved in doing what you can to notify, support, advise, act where appropriate, and hold accountable those whose primary role it is to address the issue. If you don't, you all better be prepared to sink and go down with the ship!

Whose Job Is It?

Here's an interesting short story that sums up the importance of accountability—no matter whose job it is.

This is a story of four people named Everybody, Somebody, Anybody, and Nobody.

There was an important job to be done and Everybody was asked to do it. Everybody was sure Somebody would do it. Anybody could have done it, but Nobody did it.

Somebody got angry about that because it was Everybody's job. Everybody thought Anybody could do it, but Nobody realized that Everybody wouldn't do it.

It ended that Everybody blamed Somebody when Nobody did what Anybody could have done.

As you look at yourself, your Accountability Partner, and your team, circle how often you say "It's Not My Job" as the reason for your problems/struggles/losses.

Self Rating:	Never	Seldom	Sometimes	Often	Always
AP Rating:	Never	Seldom	Sometimes	Often	Always
Team Rating:	Never	Seldom	Sometimes	Often	Always

4. Denial

Some athletes and coaches attempt to deny problems exist. They refuse to address the issues because, in their minds, admitting the problem only makes it worse. So they try to pretend it doesn't exist or isn't that bad. Denial often happens when a teammate's overactive social life has become a distraction for the team—but the athlete doesn't see it that way or want to admit it. If left unchecked, your teammate can soon get themselves in some serious trouble, cause a black eye for your whole team, and get your team on ESPN's SportsCenter for all the wrong reasons.

Coaches also can sometimes be in denial about issues that you know affect your program behind the scenes. Rather than having the courage to address these issues, they try to stick their heads in the sand, diagram some more X's and O's, and hope the problem will magically disappear. I have seen way too many seasons derailed and destroyed because coaches (and captains) tried to deny culture and chemistry problems within the team. Accountable Teammates and coaches and captains keep close tabs on the team and proactively explore and confront any potentially disruptive or divisive issues. They know that catching issues when they are small and nipping them in the bud is the best way to prevent bigger issues from blowing up the whole team.

> "You cannot escape the responsibility of tomorrow
> by evading it today."
>
> **Abraham Lincoln**

As you look at yourself and your team, circle how often you try to deny the problems/struggles/losses.

Self Rating:	Never	Seldom	Sometimes	Often	Always
AP Rating:	Never	Seldom	Sometimes	Often	Always
Team Rating:	Never	Seldom	Sometimes	Often	Always

5. Cover Up

Sometimes athletes and coaches know there is a problem but they do their best to cover it up. As they say, it is rarely the actual crime that is the biggest problem but the attempt to cover it up. When you attempt to sugarcoat, hide, or outright lie about issues to keep them from your teammates and coaches you might be successful for a while. However, usually these issues fester like fungus, multiply like mold, and eventually explode in your face if not dealt with in a timely and constructive manner. There is only so much dirt you can sweep under your team's carpet before it becomes too lumpy and people start twisting their ankles on it.

Accountable Teammates don't hide things from each other and the coaching staff. They invest the time to find out exactly what is happening and keep tabs on the team. If there is a potential concern, they alert the right people, at the right time, and in the right way about it while still preserving the confidential discussions they might have had with others.

> "The most crucial aspect of communicating: telling the truth.
> Lying and quibbling are unnecessary impediments to working as a
> team. Face-to-face communication and truth should serve as
> the basis of all team communication."

Mike Krzyzewski, Duke Men's Basketball Coach

As you look at yourself, your Accountability Partner, and your team, circle how often you try to hide and cover up your problems/struggles/issues.

Self Rating:	Never	Seldom	Sometimes	Often	Always
AP Rating:	Never	Seldom	Sometimes	Often	Always
Team Rating:	Never	Seldom	Sometimes	Often	Always

6. Confusion

Some athletes claim confusion as the source of their failure. They say they were confused about the strategy, confused about their role, confused about the signal or call, confused about the practice time, etc. Rather than being accountable for proactively clearing up any confusion they might have, they opt to put the onus on their coach or teammate for not communicating clearly enough. Obviously both sides need to be accountable when there is legitimate confusion in a player's mind or on the team itself. Both sides need to actively avoid and clarify situations where there is confusion, rather than let it slide. But using confusion as a cop out is not acceptable nor being accountable.

WEEK 4

As you look at yourself, your Accountability Partner, and your team, circle how often you cite confusion as the reason for your problems/struggles/losses.

Self Rating:	Never	Seldom	Sometimes	Often	Always
AP Rating:	Never	Seldom	Sometimes	Often	Always
Team Rating:	Never	Seldom	Sometimes	Often	Always

All of these are examples of excuses that athletes and sometimes coaches use to try to excuse their mistakes, errors, screw ups, problems, losses, failures, bad grades, etc. They minimize or eliminate their own accountability for the negative result by trying to shift the blame and dump it on to some one else. Few people buy it and no one respects it.

HOLD ME ACCOUNTABLE

OWN YOUR OUTCOMES BY PLAYING THE CLAIM GAME—
"I'M ACCOUNTABLE"

Ultimately, accountability is all about owning your outcomes—all of them. The Good. The Bad. And especially the Ugly. It means claiming and owning the results you caused, contributed to, or condoned in some way. It's easy to own your outcomes when you win and achieve success. But Accountable Teammates and leaders own the outcomes all the time—especially when they are negative. Especially when they're ugly. Especially when the "stuff" hits the fan. As President Harry Truman said, "The buck stops here." They refuse to Play the Blame and instead Play the Claim Game by being responsible, accountable, transparent, clear, truthful, and remorseful.

> "Ninety-nine percent of the failures come from people who have
> the habit of making excuses."
>
> **George Washington Carver, American Inventor**

Playing The Blame Game vs.	Playing The Claim Game.
It's not my fault	That's on me
Don't look at me	Hold me accountable
That's not my job	I need to step up
I'm not in charge	Not on my watch
I'm confused	I must clarify what's expected
No one told me it would be a problem	I need to ask first
But I didn't cause it	I didn't cause it but refuse to condone it
I thought someone else would do it	I'm responsible for getting it done
I've done what I could	How else can I help?
No one will ever find out	I need to be honest and transparent
How can I best avoid this problem?	How can I best alleviate this problem?
I've gotta find an excuse	I've gotta find a way

WEEK
4

Accountable Teammates refuse to Play the Blame Game and fully commit to Play the Claim Game. They step up, acknowledge their responsibility to get the job done and their accountability to their teammates and coaches. They own the situation, seek out constructive criticism to learn from it, and do everything they can to deliver the expected and agreed upon results next time.

Accountable Teammates apologize to the team and any others they might have affected for letting them down and not meeting the team's expectations and standards. Accountable Teammates also assure people that they will analyze, learn from it, fix it, and do everything in their power to ensure that it won't happen again. They honestly and humbly, yet assuredly tell their teammates, "It's my fault. I accept responsibility and apologize for letting you down. I will analyze it, fix it, and do everything I possibly can not to let it happen again. You have my word."

> "I didn't play well. I didn't make enough game-changing plays that I know I'm capable of making, and I felt like I let my teammates down."

LeBron James, NBA Superstar

People who adopt this accountable mindset, say these responsible things, and practice these respectable behaviors are the ones you want in your Fox Hole. These are the people you want to go to battle with. These are the people you know will have your back. These are the people you admire, respect, and trust as leaders. These are the people who are fully Accountable Teammates.

CHAPTER 4

· ·

EXTRA CREDIT ENRICHMENT EXERCISES

1. Can your teammates and coaches count on you as one of these accountable people? (circle)

Yes Sir/Ma'am   No Sir/Ma'am   No Excuse, Sir/Ma'am
If not, what will you do to own/fix it?

_____

_____

_____

_____

_____

_____

_____

2. Did your favorite sports team Play the Blame or Claim Game in their most recent loss? How?

WEEK
4

_____

_____

_____

_____

_____

_____

_____

TEAM MEETING NOTES

What are your Top 3-5 Biggest Takeaways and Action Items from this chapter?

1. _____
_____
_____

2. _____
_____
_____

3. _____
_____
_____

4. _____
_____
_____

5. _____
_____
_____

Which three people on your team do the best job of Eliminating Excuses? Why?

1. _____
_____
_____

2. _____
_____
_____

3. _____
_____
_____

Next Meeting Date:_____Time: _____

ACCOUNTABILITY PARTNER WEEKLY FEEDBACK SHEET—MODULE 5

Accountability Partner Name: _____

Date: _____

What exactly is expected/needed of you and how can you best contribute to the team this week?

My Responsibility/Role/ Expectation/ Job this Week:	Impacts Whom?	Positive/Negative Consequences	Due Date?	Results Delivered?
				Yes or No
				Yes or No
				Yes or No
				Yes or No
				Yes or No
				Yes or No

AP Challenge: _____

(Which task can you put a fun/measurable consequence on with your AP if you deliver results?)

At the end of the week, have your Accountability Partner rate you on how accountable you were:

1. How well did he/she own and execute his/her responsibilities and role this week?

   1   2   3   4   5   6   7   8   9   10

2. How well did he/she recognize and respect his/her Ripple Effect?

   1   2   3   4   5   6   7   8   9   10

3. How well did he/she consider the consequences on others before acting?

   1   2   3   4   5   6   7   8   9   10

4. How well did he/she eliminate excuses?

   1   2   3   4   5   6   7   8   9   10

5. How well did he/she have your back as your Accountability Partner?

   1   2   3   4   5   6   7   8   9   10

6. How will did he/she keep his/her commitments and deliver results?

   1   2   3   4   5   6   7   8   9   10

Comments:

_____

_____

_____

_____

CHAPTER 5

HAVE YOUR TEAMMATE'S BACK

> *When you're part of a team, you stand up for your teammates. Your loyalty is to them. You protect them through good and bad. Because they'd do the same for you.*

Yogi Berra, New York Yankees

Imagine hanging 45 feet up in the air on a jagged rock wall, clinging by your fingertips to a razor-thin edge… If you've ever gone rock climbing, you know how critical it is for someone to belay you and have your back, both literally and figuratively, in case you fall. Belaying, if you aren't familiar with the term or concept, is when a person on the ground accepts full accountability for your safety by holding on to a rope attached to your harness to catch you if you fall. As a climber high up off the ground, your life is completely in your belayer's hands. If you fall from high up on the wall, the belayer holding your rope catches you, has your back, and prevents you from falling to the ground and seriously injuring or killing yourself. At least that's how it's supposed to work…

However, my daughter Jillian, an experienced and competitive rock climber, found herself in this exact situation, 45 feet in the air, high above the ground below. As she reached for a difficult move, she fell. Tragically, rather than catching her as she should have, her belayer erred, didn't hang on to the rope, and Jillian plummeted 45 feet straight down to the ground. She landed directly on her back with a loud and back-breaking thud. She was rushed to the Duke Trauma Center in critical condition where doctors discovered she broke three vertebrae in her back and her scapula. Despite falling from the height of four and a half stories flat on her back, fortunately the fall wasn't fatal, as it would have been for most people. Miraculously, she survived and suffered no damage to her spinal cord, which would have paralyzed her. We were so blessed she "only" broke her back in several places as it could have been so much worse.

I share this scary and life-threatening example with you because Jillian and her belayer learned in an excruciatingly painful way about the vital importance of having a teammate's back. Let the story of their immense pain be your gain. When someone doesn't have your back, serious harm can be done to you and your team. Belaying is the perfect metaphor for accountability because Accountable Teammates must fully support, defend, and have each other's backs. They must take seriously their role of protector and reliably be there for their teammates. Every. Single. Time. Especially when they fall.

As we mentioned at the beginning, your success and failure are intertwined with that of each of your teammates. You rise and fall together. When one rises, you all rise. When one falls, you all fall. Just as rock climbers can find themselves in very vulnerable positions when they need to have the complete trust and support of their teammates to catch them if they fall, so too can athletes from all sports be in difficult spots where they need their teammates to have their back.

> "A team is not a group of people who work together. A team is a group of people who trust each other."

> **Simon Sinek, Author of _Start with Why_**

WHO HAS YOUR BACK? THE FOX HOLE TEST

Legendary basketball coach Don Meyer did an exercise each year with his team he called the Fox Hole Test. The Fox Hole Test has you examine which teammates you would most trust with your life if you found yourself in a life and death battle.

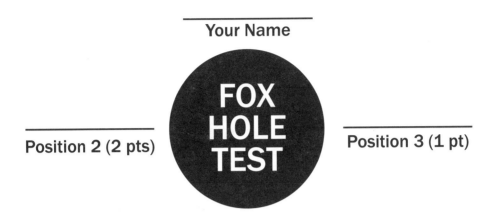

Your Name

FOX HOLE TEST

Position 2 (2 pts)

Position 3 (1 pt)

Position 1 (3 pts)

Start by writing your name at the front of the foxhole. Now consider who on your team you would want to most have your back if you were fighting a life or death battle. This should be the teammate who in your mind is the most trusted, the toughest, the most courageous, the most accountable and reliable.

The position to your left (like a left tackle in football who protects the quarterback's blindside) is the next most trusted teammate and the person to your right is the third most trusted teammate. The back position is worth 3 points, the left position is worth 2 points, and the right position is worth 1 point. You can share your ratings with your coach by texting a picture of your Fox Hole Test to him/her. Your coach can then add up all the points and come up with an All-Fox Hole Test Team of your most trusted and accountable teammates. When done honestly, the Fox Hole Test cuts through all the friendships and cliques on your team and reveals your most trusted and accountable teammates.

WEEK

5

Think about why you chose the people you did and put them in the positions you listed. What characteristics do these people possess that makes you trust them so much—that you would want them in your fox hole and having your back in a life and death situation?

_____

_____

_____

I'VE GOT YOUR 6

The Fox Hole Test also highlights what it means to have someone's back. Many in the military call this "I've Got Your 6." This phrase actually started back with World War I fighter pilots as the person in the six o'clock position (the back or bottom on the Fox Hole Test) would have the back of the fighter pilot in front of him. That too is why the person who has your back was awarded the most points in the Fox Hole Test.

> "If your teammates count on you and want to go to war with you at the toughest times, that's a characteristic that anyone should want to have."

T.J. McConnell, NBA Point Guard

WHAT IT MEANS TO HAVE YOUR TEAMMATE'S BACK

What does the phrase "I've Got Your Back" or "I've Got Your 6" mean to you? What specific things would they be doing that would clearly demonstrate they've got your back?

_____

_____

10 COMMITMENTS TO HAVE YOUR TEAMMATE'S BACK:

1. We'll sacrifice for you as we would ourselves.

2. We'll be behind you and have you covered.

3. We'll support you through the tough times.

4. We'll not talk about you behind your back.

5. We'll defend you if others criticize you.

6. We'll be there for you no matter what.

7. We'll never undermine or betray you.

8. We'll never let you be blindsided.

9. We'll pick you up when you fall.

10. We'll never leave you behind.

Each of these areas will be further explained and you should rate yourself, your Accountability Partner, and your team overall as to how well you demonstrate each of these 10 Commitments.

1. We'll sacrifice for you as we would ourselves.

Having someone's back means you will not just focus on, fight for, or worry about yourself but you will extend that exact same high-level of care, compassion, and concern to each of your teammates. It means you are as fully invested in and excited about your teammate's success as you are your own. It means you will do everything you can not to let them fail—because when they fail, you fail too. You care about them, make sacrifices for them, and watch their back as if it were your own—or someone who is near and dear to you from your own family; because the best teams are truly a family. When teammates are committed to and care about each other so much that they are not just motivated to win for themselves but also to compete and make sacrifices out of respect and love for each other, you know you have something special.

> "Your teammates are your brothers. You never want to let your family down... If you let your teammates down, there's no telling if he can trust you on the field again or not."
>
> **Urban Meyer, Ohio State Football Coach**

Self Rating:	1	2	3	4	5	6	7	8	9	10
AP Rating:	1	2	3	4	5	6	7	8	9	10
Team Rating:	1	2	3	4	5	6	7	8	9	10

2. We'll be behind you and have you covered.

We've got your back also means that we believe in you and if you happen to make a mistake, we will be there to cover for you (not cover up for you). As a team, we know you're not going to be perfect but we still support you taking intelligent and calculated risks to push yourself out of your comfort zone. If it doesn't work out we will support you and can absorb it as a team. This kind of supportive culture encourages you and your teammates to stretch and challenge yourselves because you know your teammates will be there for you.

"I believe in you. These four words can mean the difference
between a fear of failure and the courage to try."

Mike Krzyzewski, Duke Men's Basketball Coach

Self Rating:	1	2	3	4	5	6	7	8	9	10
AP Rating:	1	2	3	4	5	6	7	8	9	10
Team Rating:	1	2	3	4	5	6	7	8	9	10

3. We'll support you through the tough times.

When your teammates are in a difficult or vulnerable position, you need to be there for them. Having their back means supporting them through the inevitable tough times. A touching example of this occurred when Adriana Aviles, the four-year-old daughter of former Cleveland Indians player Mike Aviles, was diagnosed with leukemia. To show their support for their teammate and his daughter, Aviles' teammates shaved their heads. It was their way of showing their support and solidarity for Mike and Adriana because they knew that she would lose her hair with her chemo treatments. Said Cleveland manager Terry Francona, "It's a bunch of guys that really care about their teammate. A lot of the guys probably don't even know Adriana, but because it's Mikey's daughter, she's important to all of us. I think it's a way to take something that's very serious and makes you step back and think, take it and turn it into something where, I guarantee you, when she sees pictures of all these guys, she's going to smile." The clear and caring message to Adriana and her dad: We've got your back and are there for you.

Similarly, North Carolina women's soccer player Abby Elinsky lost her 23-year-old brother Nick in a fatal car crash. To show their unwavering support and love for Abby and her family, the whole team took a bus from North Carolina to Ohio to be with them for her brother's funeral. It obviously meant the world to Abby to have her team there with her as she endured the most difficult moment of her life burying her brother. When adversity and tragedy strike a teammate, be there for them. Show your concern and support in any way you possibly can. Your presence and caring means so much more than you will ever know to people during the tough times.

Self Rating:	1	2	3	4	5	6	7	8	9	10
AP Rating:	1	2	3	4	5	6	7	8	9	10
Team Rating:	1	2	3	4	5	6	7	8	9	10

10 COMMITMENTS TO HAVE YOUR TEAMMATE'S BACK

1. We'll sacrifice for you as we would ourselves.

2. We'll be behind you and have you covered.

3. We'll support you through the tough times.

4. We'll not talk about you behind your back.

5. We'll defend you if others criticize you.

6. We'll be there for you no matter what.

7. We'll never undermine or betray you.

8. We'll never let you be blindsided.

9. We'll pick you up when you fall.

10. We'll never leave you behind.

© Janssen Sports Leadership Center
Teammate's Accountability Manual
#Accountable2U

WEEK
5

4. We'll not talk about you behind your back.

If you are going to be an Accountable Teammate, you must resist gossiping about your teammates. Sure you will have frustrations with and concerns about their attitudes and behaviors from time to time, that's normal and natural. But you must not let yourself talk about them behind their backs. If you have a concern with a teammate, it is okay to talk it over with another trusted teammate provided your intent is to help and solve the situation, and as long as you are willing to talk with the person about it as well. But talking about teammates with the intent to get others to side with you is not appropriate and not the mark of an Accountable Teammate.

Stanford women's volleyball coach Kevin Hambly understands that gossip within a team can be a huge problem and highly destructive. That is why with his team he establishes a 24 Hour Rule. The 24 Hour Rule states that if a teammate voices a problem about another teammate, they both have 24 hours to address it with the teammate. If they don't constructively address the issue within 24 hours, they both are held accountable for not productively communicating and solving the issue. You should strongly consider adopting a similar standard with your program.

Self Rating:	1	2	3	4	5	6	7	8	9	10
AP Rating:	1	2	3	4	5	6	7	8	9	10
Team Rating:	1	2	3	4	5	6	7	8	9	10

5. We'll defend you if others criticize you.

In addition to your own team setting, you will likely find yourself in situations where others from outside your team may criticize a teammate. You might find a friend talking about one of your teammates because of their poor attitude. You might hear a parent criticizing one of your teammates for their poor play. You might hear a staff member at your school questioning or criticizing your coach's decision or strategy. Many times people make these critical remarks in an effort to draw you in in hopes that you will agree with them and reveal even more dirt and dissension on your own team. While there may be some truth to their statements, you don't want to throw your teammates and coaches under the bus and validate the outsider's comments. Not only is it disloyal to your teammates and coaches, it can rip apart your team and destroy your trust and credibility if it gets back to them. Simply state, "We win as a team and lose as a team and we are always trying to get better as a team," and look to change the subject on to something more positive.

Self Rating:	1	2	3	4	5	6	7	8	9	10
AP Rating:	1	2	3	4	5	6	7	8	9	10
Team Rating:	1	2	3	4	5	6	7	8	9	10

6. We'll be there for you no matter what.

No matter what happens to them, you will be there for your teammates. Your teammates will never face a difficult situation alone because you will be by their side. They know they can count on you. This kind of unwavering and unconditional support for a person is super comforting and motivating. Accountable Teammates build a sacred bond with each other where they don't want to let each other down. They promise to be there for their teammates no matter what. Their commitment to achieving results is as strong as their commitment to each other.

> "Our tradition calls for a commitment to accountability. This is not an assumption—this is a promise that I will be there for you; and I can count on you being there for me."
>
> **Bob Ladouceur, Legendary De La Salle Football Coach**

Self Rating:	1	2	3	4	5	6	7	8	9	10
AP Rating:	1	2	3	4	5	6	7	8	9	10
Team Rating:	1	2	3	4	5	6	7	8	9	10

7. We'll never undermine or betray you.

Last but certainly not least, being an Accountable Teammate means you will never do anything to undermine or betray a teammate. This is the ultimate form of disloyalty and is the quickest way to destroy a team from dissension within. This kind of calculated betrayal completely and often irreparably destroys trust. When disloyalty occurs, everyone becomes continually concerned about their own back because they are worried about having a knife stuck in it by their own "teammate"—rather than focusing on doing their job well or protecting the back of a teammate.

Sure there will be times when you might get a little jealous of a teammate who has a starting spot ahead of you or gets more coach, fan, and/or media attention than you. Human nature makes it easy to be envious of people on your own team, but as a loyal teammate, you must rise above your own petty jealousy and support them and your team 100%. If you find yourself secretly or actively rooting against one of your own teammates, you need to work it out in your own mind or with them quickly.

> "Far better to have 1000 enemies outside the tent
> than one inside the tent."

Arabic Proverb

Self Rating:	1	2	3	4	5	6	7	8	9	10
AP Rating:	1	2	3	4	5	6	7	8	9	10
Team Rating:	1	2	3	4	5	6	7	8	9	10

8. We'll never let you be blindsided.

Teammates who have their teammate's back won't let them be blindsided by opponents, issues, or problems. Oftentimes your teammates will need to be intently focused on their specific responsibilities and roles and won't be able to see all the things coming at them in their periphery or from behind that could harm or injure them. Just as a left tackle protects a quarterback from being blindsided by a blitzing linebacker in football, or a teammate calls out a back screen in basketball, or a back tells a midfielder "man on" in soccer, so too are you the helpful eyes and ears for your teammates when they can't see danger approaching. You refuse to let them be blindsided by opponents in your sport but you also make sure they aren't blindsided by situations in life as well. You will keep teammates informed of issues that might impact them.

Self Rating:	1	2	3	4	5	6	7	8	9	10
AP Rating:	1	2	3	4	5	6	7	8	9	10
Team Rating:	1	2	3	4	5	6	7	8	9	10

9. We'll pick you up if you fall.

Having someone's back means picking them up physically and mentally when they fall and fail. One of the things I love most about Championship Cultures is how they so strongly and visibly support a fallen teammate. When someone falls to the floor because they dove for a loose ball, made a tough tackle, ran into a fence trying to catch a foul ball, or just plain flubbed up and made a mistake, you see practically the whole team sprint over to help them up. This kind of speedy, enthusiastic, and unconditional support for teammates who make sacrifices for the team is a great example of having your teammate's back. It unmistakably communicates that we appreciate your effort, value your contribution, and are there immediately to pick you up when you fall. Establish a team standard and make a pact with each other that you will always sprint over to help up a fallen teammate whenever possible. It sends a clear message to them and everyone else that you've got their back.

Self Rating:	1	2	3	4	5	6	7	8	9	10
AP Rating:	1	2	3	4	5	6	7	8	9	10
Team Rating:	1	2	3	4	5	6	7	8	9	10

10. We will never leave you behind.

Having your teammate's back means you will never leave them—period - especially if they are in a difficult or dangerous situation. If a teammate gets caught up in a fight, you will protect them and get them out of the situation ASAP. If a fight occurs, think "evacuate" vs. "escalate". Evacuate means quickly and safely getting them out of the situation. Escalate means jumping into the fight with them and making matters much worse for you and them. It's just not worth it.

If a teammate is lured into a dangerous situation at a party, evacuate them. If a teammate wants to get into a car with someone who has had too much to drink, evacuate them. If a teammate wants to walk home alone, evacuate them. Teammates don't let teammates get into dangerous situations—and if they somehow do, they evacuate them as quickly and as safely as possible. Make a promise and pact to never leave your teammates behind at a party, in a fight, or in any situation where they could get hurt in any way. No one left behind! Evacuate them.

> "Family means no one gets left behind or forgotten."
>
> **David Ogden Stiers, Actor**

Self Rating:	1	2	3	4	5	6	7	8	9	10
AP Rating:	1	2	3	4	5	6	7	8	9	10
Team Rating:	1	2	3	4	5	6	7	8	9	10

Yes, being a Great Teammate and consistently having each other's back is hard! It takes a lot of effort, compassion, communication, listening, understanding, empathy, and maturity. But being a Great Teammate creates such a positive and productive culture within your team that it is definitely worth it.

Add up your points on the previous 10 Commitments to see how well you, your Accountability Partner, and your team have each other's back. See what grade you have earned.

Self Score _____ Grade _____

AP Score _____ Grade _____

Team Score _____ Grade _____

SCORE GRADE AND COMMENTS

90-100 A—your teammates and coaches highly trust you to have their back

80-89   B—you do a good job having your team's back but have some areas to improve

70-79   C—you need to do a better job having your teammates' and coaches' back

60-69   D—your teammates and coaches likely don't have much trust in you

10-59   F—your teammates and coaches don't trust you, you need to earn it quickly!

1. Which two specific commitments are your biggest strengths?

_____

_____

2. Which two commitments do you need to improve to be more accountable to your team?

_____

_____

3. Which two specific commitments are your Accountability Partner's biggest strengths?

_____

_____

4. Which two specific commitments does your Accountability Partner need to improve?

_____

_____

5. Which two specific commitments are your team's biggest strengths?

_____

_____

6. Which two commitments does your team need to improve to build a Culture of Accountability?

_____

_____

CHAPTER 5
· ·
EXTRA CREDIT ENRICHMENT EXERCISES

1. Create a special Shield Award to honor those athletes who best have their teammates' back during the week.

2. Former Florida State football coach Bobby Bowden challenged his team to Hold the Rope. Coach Bowden says, "What does holding the rope mean? You are hanging from the edge of a cliff five hundred yards in the air. The only thing between you and falling to the ground is a piece of rope with the person of your choice on the other end. Who do you know that you can trust enough? Who do you know who has enough guts to withstand rope burn, watch blood drip from his hands, and still not let go? Look around and ask, 'Who can I trust to hold the rope?' Who will let his hands bleed for me? If you can look at every member of your team and say they will hold the rope, then your team will win!" You can use this "Hold the Rope" example with your team and challenge everyone to hold the rope for each other and have each other's back.

TEAM MEETING NOTES

What are your Top 3-5 Biggest Takeaways and Action Items from this chapter?

1. _____

_____

_____

2. _____

_____

_____

3. _____

_____

_____

4. _____

_____

_____

5. _____

_____

_____

Which three people on your team do the best job of Having Your Teammate's Back? Why?

1. _____

_____

_____

2. _____

_____

_____

3. _____

_____

_____

Next Meeting Date:_____Time: _____

ACCOUNTABILITY PARTNER WEEKLY FEEDBACK SHEET—MODULE 6

Accountability Partner Name: _____

Date: _____

What exactly is expected/needed of you and how can you best contribute to the team this week?

My Responsibility/Role/ Expectation/ Job this Week:	Impacts Whom?	Positive/Negative Consequences	Due Date?	Results Delivered?
				Yes or No
				Yes or No
				Yes or No
				Yes or No
				Yes or No
				Yes or No

AP Challenge: _____

(Which task can you put a fun/measurable consequence on with your AP if you deliver results?)

At the end of the week, have your Accountability Partner rate you on how accountable you were:

1. How well did he/she own and execute his/her responsibilities and role this week?

    1   2   3   4   5   6   7   8   9   10

2. How well did he/she recognize and respect his/her Ripple Effect?

    1   2   3   4 ,   5   6   7   8   9   10

3. How well did he/she consider the consequences on others before acting?

    1   2   3   4   5   6   7   8   9   10

4. How well did he/she eliminate excuses?

    1   2   3   4   5   6   7   8   9   10

5. How well did he/she have your back as your Accountability Partner?

    1   2   3   4   5   6   7   8   9   10

6. How will did he/she keep his/her commitments and deliver results?

    1   2   3   4   5   6   7   8   9   10

Comments:

_____

_____

_____

_____

WEEK

5

CHAPTER 6
KEEP YOUR COMMITMENTS AND DELIVER RESULTS

> " *You are what you do. Not what you say you'll do.* "
>
> **Carl Jung, Psychologist**

Being an Accountable Teammate means your teammates and coaches can consistently rely on you to keep your commitments and deliver much-needed results for the team. For you, failure is just not an option and you will persist until the job is done. If you can't consistently follow through on your word and competently fulfill your responsibilities and role, you will quickly lose your teammates' and coaches' trust and respect and be considered unreliable in their eyes.

WEEK
6

KEEP YOUR COMMITMENTS

As we discussed in the beginning, as a teammate you have certain responsibilities that you are expected to commit to and fulfill for your team. When you consistently and reliably keep your commitments and agreements, you earn trust. The two best ways to become an Accountable Athlete are to:

1.   Do What You Say You Will Do

2.   Apologize and Make It Right When You Don't

DO WHAT YOU SAY YOU WILL DO

You have to remember that your word is your bond. If you tell someone you will be there, be there on time, if not early. If you tell your coach you will get the job done, then make plays consistently. If you tell your instructor you will have the assignment completed and turned in on time before you leave on a trip for an away game, turn it in on time. Accountability is doing what you say you will do—not necessarily because you have to, but because you want to out of honor and respect for keeping your word with your teammates, coaches, teachers, etc. Doing what you say you will do consistently, cheerfully, and dependably means people can rely on you.

- Doing what you say you will do 1 time provides hope.

- Doing what you say you will do 10 times builds confidence.

- Doing what you say you will do 100 times builds trust.

- Doing what you say you will do 1000 times is accountability.

If you don't follow through and do the things you say you will and are expected of you, you will quickly and sometimes irreparably destroy your own credibility and damage your teammates' and coaches' faith in you. This is especially true if you are considered a team leader or have the title of one. As a leader you need to be the best example of the championship attitudes and actions you expect of your teammates.

YOU'VE GOT TO PULL YOUR WEIGHT

Keeping commitments is about unfailingly pulling your weight. You've got to follow through and do the things your team relies on you to do. When you don't pull your weight, your teammates and coaches are forced to pick up the slack for you. They already have their own weight to bear so adding yours puts an extra and unnecessary burden on them to carry you. Imagine playing your sport with a teammate on your back. Imagine running sprints with a teammate on your back. Imagine having to add your teammate on the barbell when you lift. In essence, when a teammate doesn't fulfill their responsibilities, play their role, and do their job, it's like you now have to carry them on your own back to get their job done and yours.

Unkept commitments, unmet expectations, and broken agreements quickly erode trust and will be a significant source of strain and frustration for both your teammates and coaches. Your team will quickly learn that they really can't count on you because of your empty promises.

Thus, don't say you can do something and commit to it unless you know for sure you have the ability, motivation, and time to get it done. Don't set yourself and your team up for failure on the front end if you know you can't follow through and keep your commitment. Better to honestly state your concerns about making the commitment on the front end than to not follow through and lose respect on the back end.

Finally, outright lying and making up excuses about why you failed to follow through is obviously a huge problem and clear violation of your team's trust. If you should find yourself in a bind about keeping a commitment, the best thing to do is to own up to it and follow the advice below.

IF IT'S IMPOSSIBLE TO KEEP A COMMITMENT APOLOGIZE AND MAKE IT RIGHT/BETTER

Even though you will do your absolute best to keep all your commitments, of course there will be some rare situations when you will not be able to follow through on them. This might be because something extremely out of the ordinary came up last minute that you couldn't have foreseen or a family emergency occurred. If for some reason you can't keep a commitment, let the key people affected by it know as early as possible, sincerely apologize for not being able to keep your commitment and explain your reason why, and ideally try to find a solution or agreeable substitute for any problems that might be caused by not following through on your commitment.

If you can't keep a commitment:

1. Communicate it—as soon as realistically possible, make sure anyone and everyone it impacts knows you are struggling to keep a commitment so they can adjust accordingly

2. Own it—take full responsibility and accountability for it rather than making up any kind of excuse or blaming someone or something else

3. Apologize for it—sincerely express your apologies and regret that you are not able to follow through on your word and what was expected

4. Make it right/better—do whatever you can to make up for your unfulfilled commitment by going the extra mile and either finding an agreeable substitute or do something even better than what was expected

For example, let's say your team commits to participate in a community service event in your area. However, a severe storm of some kind comes in and makes it far too dangerous for you to safely get there. Of course you would call the organizer, apologize for not being able to make your commitment, and reschedule at the soonest workable time for both groups. If possible, you could even double the time you would have spent with them in order to make it right. To be an Accountable Teammate, keeping your commitments is absolutely essential.

ACCOUNTABLE TEAMMATES DELIVER RESULTS

In addition to keeping commitments, your teammates and coaches also depend on you to deliver high-level, consistent results based on your particular role. To consider you accountable, they need you to competently do your job for the good of the entire team day in and day out. If you haven't figured it out already, let me be crystal clear: sports revolve primarily around delivering winning results, especially the higher up you go. That's why there are scoreboards, statistics, trophies, and awards. They all measure and reward those who deliver results.

If you can deliver results, you play, become a starter, make the all conference team, get trophies, receive media attention, earn a scholarship, get drafted, and sign endorsement deals as you move up the ranks. If you can't consistently deliver the necessary results in your sport, you either don't make the team or you sit the bench and actively support someone who can. It's as simple as that. Your teammates and coaches count on you to produce in your role, no matter what it might be. If you can't deliver the necessary results, they find someone else who can do the job to take your place and make the critical contributions to the team. Sports are largely a meritocracy where results rule; those who produce play and those who don't produce don't play.

RESULTS RULE
If you produce -> you play
If you don't produce -> you don't play

The Value of Delivering Results: A Message to Garcia

One of the best stories about the supreme value of delivering results without excuses is an essay by Elbert Hubbard called *A Message to Garcia*. It's a true story that occurred way back in 1899 but is just as true and relevant today.

Facing a looming war with Spain, President William McKinley desperately needed to get an urgent message to General Calixto Garcia in Cuba, who was leading the Cuban fight for independence against Spain. Because the Spanish army was relentlessly hunting him, General Garcia hid out deep in the mountains of Cuba—so no one knew of his exact whereabouts. However, for the success of this operation, President McKinley had to get a top-secret message quickly and safely delivered to General Garcia, or the whole country and their fight for independence would be in great peril and the U.S. would be at war with Spain.

President McKinley met with Colonel Arthur Wagner, the head of the Military Intelligence for the United States, and with great seriousness in his voice asked him, "Where can I find a man who will carry a message to Garcia?" Colonel Wagner had no hesitation whatsoever in his answer. "I have a man, a young officer, Lieutenant Andrew Summers Rowan. If anybody can get a message to Garcia, Rowan can." "Send him!" was the President's order.

Colonel Wagner quickly found Lieutenant Rowan and told him of the President's urgent and essential mission. "Young man, you must carry a message to General Garcia, who will be found somewhere in the eastern part of Cuba. You must plan and act for yourself. The task is yours and yours only. There must be no failure on your part." Colonel Wagner looked at Rowan intently, shook his hand, and repeated, "Get that message to Garcia." Without asking one question, Rowan set out immediately for Cuba to find General Garcia.

Rowan considered his highly dangerous and urgent mission, "In instances of this kind, where one's reputation, as well as his life, is at stake, it is usual to ask for written instructions… But in this case it never occurred to me to ask for written instructions; my sole thought was that I was charged with getting a message to Garcia and to get from him certain information and that I was going to do it."

Completely on his own, Rowan took a train from Washington, D.C. to New York, where he boarded a boat to Jamaica. In Jamaica, Rowan secretly met with a group of Cuban rebels who told him they could help him find General Garcia. He quickly yet carefully made his way through the jungles of Jamaica until he came to a small fishing boat that would stealthy take him to Cuba, 100 miles to the north.

Rowan said, "I have no hesitation in saying that there were some anxious

WEEK

6

moments for me following our departure. . . My life would be at stake if I should be caught within three miles of the Cuban coast. . . Capture meant death and my failure to carry my message to Garcia. But I must succeed; I must find Garcia and deliver my message!"

Sure enough, as they were about three miles from the Cuban shore, their worst nightmare came true. A Spanish military boat spotted them and approached at a high rate of speed, guns pointed. Rowan quickly hid and the crew dropped their sail and tried to pretend they were fishing in hopes the Spanish would be fooled.

As the Spanish military boat came up along side, the ship's commander cried out in a loud voice, "Catching anything?" Fortunately the Spanish were fooled into thinking Rowan's crew was merely fishing and continued on their way patrolling the waters.

Rowan and his crew made it to the Cuban shore where they met another group of rebels, who would try to sneak them through the hot and humid rain forests and up into the mountains in hopes the Spanish cavalry would not detect them and kill them. Despite some very close calls, Rowan and his crew were able to elude the Spanish military and make it several miles inland to General Garcia's hideout. After nine days in harrowing and life-threatening conditions and traveling over one thousand miles by boat, foot, and horseback, Rowan finally reached General Garcia and delivered his mission-critical message.

Rowan said, "I was in the presence of General Garcia. The long and toilsome journey with its many risks, its chances of failure, its chances for death, was over. I had succeeded." Rowan indeed succeeded, not only for himself, but for General Garcia, the Cuban people, and the United States as well.

Elbert Hubbard, the author of *A Message to Garcia*, writes, "Rowan delivered the message to Garcia and the response got back to McKinley without Rowan ever asking, 'Where is he? What does he look like? Who are his contacts? How do I get there?' He simply took the orders and did what he was asked to do.

Is there a Rowan among us? Is there somebody who can get a message to Garcia without having to do an interrogation of his senior officer first? Is there someone who can get the job done without needing to have his employer hold his hand until the task is completed? If not, the boss might as well do it himself. Is there somebody that I can just ask to accomplish a task, and the next time I see them I am told, 'I'm finished with that. What do you want me to do next?' Where can I find someone like that? Where is he? Can I find a Rowan? Is there someone who can get a message to Garcia? They are out there. There's just not enough of them. There are probably some Rowans reading this right now. There will always be a few of those individuals who are extraordinary.

Extraordinary means above ordinary. Those who don't just do what is expected of them; they surpass the expectations of others, in their pursuit of excellence.

People haven't changed in the last 100 years, have they? Every time I give someone a task and they start asking me a hundred questions, I immediately say to myself, 'This poor soul could not get a message to Garcia.'"

Plain and simple, Rowan delivered results and was highly valued for it. He was completely accountable to the president and his country and delivered the all-important message to Garcia.

Can you do the same for your team? Can you, in essence, deliver a message to Garcia?

Yes, Sir   No, Sir   No Excuse, Sir   I do not understand, Sir

ACCOUNTABLE TEAMMATES DELIVER

Accountable Teammates consistently deliver winning results, no matter what the obstacles, opponent, or adversity. For them, failure is just not an option. They reliably get the message to Garcia. They meet and exceed expectations. They make things happen. They get things done. They make plays. They move the needle. They produce. Consistently. Reliably. Like clockwork. All day. Every day. Without question. Without delay. Without excuse. Done. Next!

Coaches love all aspects of Accountable Teammates but especially their ability to reliably produce results for the team. They love that they are so acCOUNTable—meaning they can consistently count on them. If you can be one of these Accountable Teammates where you dependably deliver high-level results, I virtually guarantee your coach will find a spot for you.

> "I do my best because I'm counting on you counting on me."

> **Maya Angelou, Poet**

Of course, producing results also has an important ethical component to it as well. Assuming your program places a premium on character and integrity, as it should, you need to produce results within the rules of your team, the game, and your own moral compass. This is not a win at all costs proposition or a "by any means necessary" unethical operation—but producing results with honor and integrity; means you can be proud of and your team can be proud of.

WEEK

6

TO DELIVER RESULTS YOU'VE GOT TO KNOW AND HIT YOUR NUMBERS

What does it mean to produce results? One obvious way to produce winning results for your team is to look at the stats. Every sport has some critical statistical

ACCOUNTABLE TEAMMATES DELIVER RESULTS

numbers that are key for the whole team winning—as well as determining the individual roles within the team.

Let's take basketball for example. According to *Basketball on Paper* author Dean Oliver, who has statistically analyzed tens of thousands of basketball games, the team that almost always wins the game is the one that wins the battles in these key stats:

- Better Offensive Shooting Percentage (wins 79% of time)

- Less Turnovers (wins 69% of time)

- Less Fouls (wins 67% of time)

- More Offensive Rebounds (wins 63% of time)

When teams can deliver results in one of these key areas they statistically increase their chances of winning. When they can deliver results in two or three of these areas, they dramatically increase their chances of winning. And when they can deliver results on all four of these critical areas, they virtually assure themselves of winning.

Similarly, Notre Dame Baseball monitors and measures the number of Quality At Bats (QAB) their players have because they know that QABs lead to guys getting on base, scoring runs, and winning games. They define and determine a QAB as "an at-bat that makes a positive contribution toward our team goals" and includes any of these 8 elements:

1. Hard Barrel Contact

2. Family First At Bat (sacrifice bunt or fly)

3. Hit By Pitch

4. Base on Balls

5. 8 Plus Pitch At Bat

6. Score a Run Any Way

7. Two Strike Hits

8. 4+ Pitches After 0-2 Count

Their goal as a team is to have a .500 QAB average.

What are the key numbers and stats in your sport that most often determine winning?

_____

_____

_____

TEAM RESULTS BOARD

In fact, many teams like North Carolina men's basketball have a board in their locker room that shows how well they have won the key battles within the game for each competition. Battles they win get a sticker or team logo placed over them and battles they lose are left blank. It is easy then to hold the entire team accountable to focus on and win the key battles.

TEACH, TRAIN, TALLY, AND TRACK RESULTS

The best way to get your teammates to accountably produce more winning results for your team is to follow this four-step process:

Step 1: Teach the Results

Teach your teammates about the key results areas in your sport and on your team based on your system and core values. Let them know what numbers are critical for your team to hit and why. They should know your key results numbers so well that if you woke them at 4:00 in the morning they would be able to recite them.

How well does your team understand the key results areas for your team's success?

1   2   3   4   5   6   7   8   9   10

Step 2: Train for Results

Train in such a way that your practices, workouts, conditioning, etc., all work to improve these key numbers. If rebounding is key for your team, then make sure you focus on effectively boxing out, do lots of rebounding drills, and hit the weight room to develop your upper and lower body strength.

How well does your team train for results and focus on the key areas for your team's success?

1   2   3   4   5   6   7   8   9   10

Step 3: Tally the Results

Don't just do drills that focus on your key area but find a way to quantify them. Tally the number of successes in a drill or record how much time it takes to successfully complete it. Of course you will also tally key stats within the competition itself. Legendary coach Pat Summitt of Tennessee women's basketball would tally key stats for her team and have a manager write them up in the locker room at halftime before the players even got in. Tallying not only holds people accountable for their results because they know they are being monitored because their performance matters, it also increases the intensity, focus, and competitiveness of your drills and games as well.

How well does your team measure the key results areas in your practices and competition?

1   2   3   4   5   6   7   8   9   10

Step 4: Track the Results

Don't just tally the results once but track how well you and your team meet them over time. Whenever possible, track the results in real-time, make sure they are 100% accurate, and post them in a visible spot where the people who are responsible for them can see them often. Look for trends and hopefully your team is on an upward trajectory overall in your key results areas. Sports and life is a matter of a constant never-ending ascension—so look to improve upon your individual and team results over time. You can post your high scores not only for this year's team but include the records throughout the history of the program so people can look to leave a legacy of being an all-time great.

How well does your team track your key results areas over time to see trends?

1   2   3   4   5   6   7   8   9   10

Knowing, focusing on, and delivering these numbers is obviously a highly critical part of being successful. Thus, if you want to help your team win, gain your coach's trust, and earn more playing time, it would be super smart for you to focus on delivering these key numbers for your team in practices, scrimmages, and of course, competitions.

TALLYING AND TRACKING YOUR INDIVIDUAL RESULTS

Taking this a logical next step to the individual level, you can do the same thing on an personal level. Talk with your coach to pinpoint the key stats for your sport that help you win the competition, especially based on your particular team's strategy. Then look at your specific role and come up with the key numbers that you need to hit to best contribute to your team's success.

For example, if you aspire to be a leadoff hitter in baseball or softball, your On Base Percentage is key. If you can get on base 35% of the time in baseball and 45% of the time in softball, you deliver some fantastic results.

For basketball, if you are a guard, you would want to shoot a high percentage of at least 45%, have a great assist to turnover ratio of 3:1, force your defender into foul trouble, and harass the person you're guarding into several turnovers and shooting a low percentage. If you were a big man, you too would want to shoot a high percentage of 55%, grab 10+ rebounds a game with at least three of them being offensive, force your defender into foul trouble, and keep the person you're guarding from getting rebounds and shooting a high percentage. By knowing, focusing on, and delivering these kinds of numbers, you will virtually guarantee yourself playing time.

> What specific results must you achieve in your position and role on the team in order to contribute to your team's success?

_____

_____

TALLYING AND TRACKING YOUR ABILITY TO DELIVER RESULTS

Obviously you will need to first consistently hit these numbers in practice to prove to your coach and teammates that you also can do them in the game. North Carolina women's soccer, winners of 22 national championships, tallies and tracks every competitive drill their players are involved in and whether or not the player has won or lost. Every competition, whether it is 1v1, 2v2, or 3v3, is tallied and tracked because their effort, competitiveness, and accountability in each of these drills is so important. Obviously, the athletes who are winning most of the drills and delivering results in a competitive practice setting are also the same athletes who are earning significant time on the field on game day.

> "Players think—'Play me and I'll show you.'
> Coaches think—'Show me and I'll play you.'"
>
> **Shaka Smart, Texas Men's Basketball Coach**

Every sport has many intangibles that are hard to quantify, so everything cannot be based solely on the numbers. As the phrase goes, "Not everything that can be counted counts, and not everything that counts can be counted."

There are other important, tough-to-measure intangibles like leadership, chemistry, and culture that are important to your team's success that should not be discounted or overlooked. Yet, we have also found ways to quantify these important measures with our various evaluations (just like we did with accountability in this *Manual*) so you can factor in these intangibles as well when making decisions that impact your team.

> "You need to have that pressure upon yourself and
> others hold you accountable that you're going to score.
> That's your job as a forward."

Alex Morgan, USA Women's Soccer

TALLYING AND TRACKING RESULTS ENSURES ACCOUNTABILITY

Accountable Teammates love tallying and tracking key performance metrics because they love to compete and improve their numbers. Unaccountable athletes hate tracking because there is nowhere for them to hide. Teammates and coaches clearly see their level of performance when it is tracked and posted. They too must face up to the fact that they aren't getting the job done and peer pressure typically forces them to step up their performance or step aside. Tracking also reveals and justifies who has earned playing time. Those that produce and deliver results in practices and competition earn playing time—those that don't produce, don't play.

REWARD RESULTS

In addition to earning playing time, find fun ways to reward those who deliver key results. Since creating turnovers is such a key to winning football games, Alabama Football gives a "Ball Out Belt" to players who create them while Miami Football gives a Turnover Chain. LSU Gymnastics rewards Tiger Eyes to players who create results in and out of the gym. Think of some fun and creative ways to reward people who produce key results for your team.

ALL DAY, EVERY DAY

Finally, consistency in delivering these results is key. Most any athlete can have a great game every now and then but the ones who teammates and coaches can count on the most are the ones who consistently get the job done all day, every day. As Boston Celtics coach Brad Stevens succinctly says, "Be reliable and do your job every day."

CHAPTER 6

EXTRA CREDIT ENRICHMENT EXERCISES

1. Research what other teams and individuals do in your sport to teach, train, tally and track their key results. How can you apply these ideas to your team?

_____

_____

_____

_____

2. In consultation with your coach, create a customized Key Results Board for your team that shows how well your team delivers results in your team's key areas for each competition.

3. Create a personalized Key Results Board for yourself to track how well you consistently deliver the key results expected for your particular role.

TEAM MEETING NOTES

What are your Top 3-5 Biggest Takeaways and Action Items from this chapter?

1. _____
   _____
   _____

2. _____
   _____
   _____

3. _____
   _____
   _____

4. _____
   _____
   _____

5. _____
   _____
   _____

Which three people on your team do the best job of Keeping their
Commitments and Delivering Results? Why?

1. _____
   _____
   _____

2. _____
   _____
   _____

3. _____
   _____
   _____

Next Meeting Date:_____Time: _____

WEEK
6

CONCLUSION

Congratulations! If you have kept your commitments and been fully accountable to your teammates and coaches by completing this *Manual*, you should now have a much better understanding and appreciation for the power of accountability. More importantly, your daily attitudes and actions in practices, competition, the weight room, classroom, on campus, and in the community should now better demonstrate your accountability to your team. You've learned that accountability isn't just something you passively profess, it must be something you actively practice and demonstrate each and every day.

MEASURING YOUR PROGRESS

As a way to measure your progress from start to finish, I have included another copy of the 6 Attitudes and Actions of Accountable Teammates Evaluation on the next page. Take the short eval again to see if there are any differences from the first time you took it. Keep in mind you may have unintentionally inflated your self scores the first time you took the eval because you didn't really understand what it meant to be fully accountable to your teammates and coaches the way you do now. You are now much wiser and more sophisticated in your understanding of what it means to be accountable so your scores are likely to be more realistic and accurate at the end of the *Manual* than at the beginning.

A better indicator of your progress is often to compare your coach's rating at the start to your coach's rating at the end—as hopefully they will see some measurable progress as you have become more accountable since you started the *Manual*.

BE ACCOUNTABLE ON EVERY TEAM

The skills in this *Manual* obviously apply to your sports team—but my hope is that you also apply them to every aspect of your life. You will be a part of numerous teams as you move forward in life: sports teams, school teams, business teams, family teams, etc. Each of these teams wants and needs Accountable Teammates. So be sure to own your role, recognize your Ripple Effect, consider the consequences, eliminate excuses, have your teammate's back, keep your commitments, and deliver results for every single team you are a part of. Not only will you be considered a Great Teammate when you do this, you will also earn their respect as a team leader.

PLEASE HOLD ME ACCOUNTABLE AND SHARE YOUR FEEDBACK!

To hold me accountable so I can deliver the best results moving forward, I strongly encourage you to share your feedback on this *Manual*! Please email me your honest thoughts on the questions below at jeff@jeffjanssen.com with the subject line Accountability Manual Feedback:

1. What did you like best about this *Manual?*

2. What did you like least about this *Manual?*

3. How exactly can this *Manual* be improved?

6 ATTITUDES AND ACTIONS OF ACCOUNTABLE TEAMMATES EVALUATION

This evaluation helps you see how accountable you are to your teammates and coaches. Honestly answer the questions using the 1 (Strongly Disagree) to 10 (Strongly Agree) scale below.

> 1–2 = Strongly Disagree
> 3–4 = Disagree
> 5–6 = Neutral
> 7–8 = Agree
> 9–10 = Strongly Agree

1. **Own Your Responsibilities and Role:** I clearly understand, accept, and own my team responsibilities and role and competently and reliably fulfill them to the best of my ability.

   1   2   3   4   5   6   7   8   9   10

2. **Recognize Your Ripple Effect:** I recognize and respect the fact that my actions and attitudes affect and impact the success and reputation of my teammates, coaches, and others.

   1   2   3   4   5   6   7   8   9   10

3. **Consider the Consequences:** I consciously and carefully consider the consequences of my words and actions on my teammates, coaches, and others before I speak and act.

   1   2   3   4   5   6   7   8   9   10

4. **Eliminate Excuses:** I refuse to make excuses by blaming someone or something else for my mistakes, failures, and losses. Instead, I claim full accountability, apologize, analyze, and fix it.

   1   2   3   4   5   6   7   8   9   10

5. **Have Your Teammate's Back:** I am always there for my teammates and coaches, especially through the tough times, and do not gossip about, undermine, or betray them in any way.

   1   2   3   4   5   6   7   8   9   10

6. **Keep Your Commitments and Deliver Results:** I keep the commitments I make to my teammates and coaches and consistently deliver the high-level results they expect from me.

   1   2   3   4   5   6   7   8   9   10

Add up your total score for each of the six questions:

TOTAL SCORE _____

6 Actions of Accountable Teammates Evaluation Rating Scale

54–60— You are a highly Accountable Teammate! Teach your teammates what you know.

46–53— You are somewhat accountable with some room for improvement. Study this Manual.

38–45— You are not as accountable as you and your team need you to be. Take a lot of notes.

WEEK 6

30–37— You are not accountable and can benefit greatly from completing this Manual.

6–29— You are a highly unreliable teammate! Memorize and apply this Manual!

ABOUT THE AUTHOR

Widely considered the world's top expert on Sports Leadership, Jeff Janssen is the founder and president of the Janssen Sports Leadership Center.

Jeff and his top-notch team's pioneering work on sports leadership development with student-athletes and coaches has led to the creation of cutting edge Leadership Academies at Arkansas, Barton, Baylor, Boston University, Cary Academy, UNC-Charlotte, Charlotte Country Day, Colby, Colgate, Colorado, Concordia Lutheran, Fordham, Georgetown, George Washington, Guelph, Holy Cross, Houston, Illinois, Lafayette, Lehigh, Loyola, LSU, Michigan, New Brunswick, Notre Dame, NC State, Pitt, Santa Fe Christian, St. Francis Xavier, Stanford, Stetson, South Carolina, Wake Forest, Winston-Salem State, and Yale.

A prolific author, Jeff has authored numerous books including *The Team Captain's Leadership Manual, The Team Captain's Culture Manual, The Athlete's Responsibility Manual, The Athlete's Commitment Manual, How to Build and Sustain a Championship Culture, Championship Team Building, Jeff Janssen's Peak Performance Playbook, How to Develop Relentless Competitors, Develop Relentless Competitors Drillbook,* and *The Seven Secrets of Successful Coaches.*

Jeff and his family live in Cary, North Carolina and enjoy playing and watching sports, traveling, and reading.

www.JanssenSportsLeadership.com

ACKNOWLEDGMENTS

I would love to thank all of my "teammates" who helped to make this book possible! First, thanks to my fabulous team at the Janssen Sports Leadership Center: Greg Shelley, Becky Bedics, Julie Ammary, and Julie Domina. Thanks for your commitment to developing the world's next generation of leaders!

Thank you to all of the student-athletes, coaches, point people, and administrators at our Leadership Academies across the world. We love learning from you all about responsibility, accountability, teamwork, culture, and leadership on a regular basis!

Special thanks to the following people for reading the manuscript and providing their valuable insights and comments on the book: Skye Angus, Becky Bedics, Chad Bickley, Jonathan Crossland, Julie Domina, Kristi Janssen, Darcy McFarlane, Tom Nobles, Haley Pace, Kyle Rechlicz, Bev Smith, Jill Wilson, and Tom Hanna and Akron Volleyball. Your helpful input made this book so much better!

Thanks to Sherry Roberts and Tricia Principe for their excellent graphic design work as well as Adam Hieber and Cushing Malloy for their quality printing and customer service.

And last but certainly not least, thanks to my amazing family: Kristi, Ryan, Jillian, and Trey. Thank you for always having my back and belaying me through the ups and downs of life. I appreciate all of your love and support and am so fortunate to be a part of our Janssen Team!

REFERENCES

COACH'S INTRO

Anson Dorrance—personal communication.

Nick Saban—http://lessonsfromsports.com/three-traits-we-can-not-afford-to-lose/

Pat Summitt—*Reach for the Summit: The Definite Dozen System for Succeeding at Whatever You Do* (1999)

Lenny Wilkens—http://www.azquotes.com/quote/553243

ATHLETE'S INTRO

Peyton Manning—http://www.wiseoldsayings.com/teammates-quotes/

Derek Jeter—http://www.azquotes.com/quote/1279301

Carla Overbeck—personal communication.

Vince Wilfork—http://kwese.espn.com/boston/nfl/columns/story?columnist=reiss_mike&id=4982626

Shalane Flanagan—https://www.shape.com/fitness/tips/running-superstar-shalane-flanagans-tips-going-distance

CHAPTER 1—OWN YOUR RESPONSIBILITIES AND ROLE

Julius Peppers—http://lacrossetribune.com/sports/local/ageless-wonders/article_39f5e945-0302-5cf7-9b0c-161a0dbae641.html

Iowa State Football Code of Conduct—http://www.spongecoach.com/iowa-state-cyclone-code-of-conduct-policy/

George Bernard Shaw—https://www.brainyquote.com/quotes/george_bernard_shaw_385438

Doug Collins—http://basketballhq.com/doug-collins-coaching-u-clinic-notes

Shane Battier—https://www.theplayerstribune.com/elite-glue-guys-101/

Dr. Martin Luther King, Jr.—http://www.thekingcenter.org/blog/mlk-quote-week-all-labor-uplifts-humanity-has-dignity-and-importance-and-should-be-undertaken

Bill Belichick—http://boston.cbslocal.com/2015/01/31/patriots-reveal-layers-of-complex-meaning-of-do-your-job/

Danny Amendola—http://boston.cbslocal.com/2015/01/31/patriots-reveal-layers-of-complex-meaning-of-do-your-job/

CHAPTER 2—RECOGNIZE YOUR RIPPLE EFFECT

Mia Hamm—*Go for the Goal: A Champion's Guide to Winning in Soccer and Life* (1999)

Gregg Popovich—http://www.businessinsider.com/gregg-popovich-explains-qualities-spurs-look-for-in-players-2016-2

Dane Fife—https://twitter.com/coachdanefife/status/919981734766219265

Edgar A. Guest—*Collected Verse of Edgar Guest* (1934)

Charlie Plumb—https://www.youtube.com/watch?v=Kw2ulUDLeJc

CHAPTER 3—CONSIDER THE CONSEQUENCES

Brad Stevens—https://www.thesimpledollar.com/inspiration-from-brad-stevens-dolores-oriordan-steno-pads-and-more/

Buck Showalter—https://coachingclipboard.org/2017/09/30/being-a-good-teammate-david-price/

Joe Dumars—http://www.azquotes.com/quote/700729

Sir Edmund Burke—https://www.brainyquote.com/quotes/edmund_burke_377528

Pat Summitt—*Reach for the Summit.*

CHAPTER 4—ELIMINATE EXCUSES

Ben Franklin—http://lenderman.weebly.com/quotes.html

Kyle Maynard—*No Excuses: The True Story of a Congenital Amputee Who Became a Champion in Wrestling and in Life* (2006)

Ed Ruggerro—*Duty First: A Year in the Life of West Point and the Making of American Leaders* (2002)

Bum Phillips—https://247sports.com/Coach/3616/Quotes/You-fail-all-the-time-but-you-arent-a-failure-until-you-start-bl-35961247

Urban Meyer—*Above the Line: Lessons in Leadership and Life from a Championship Season*, p. 30-31. (2015)

Bill Parcels—http://www.azquotes.com/quote/851202

Who's Job Is It?—http://www.smart-jokes.org/everybody-somebody-anybody-and-nobody.html

Abraham Lincoln—https://www.brainyquote.com/quotes/abraham_lincoln_101733

Mike Krzyzewski—*Beyond Basketball: Coach K's Keywords for Success* (2006)

George Washington Carver—https://www.brainyquote.com/quotes/george_washington_carver_158549

LeBron James—http://articles.sun-sentinel.com/2012-06-11/sports/sfl-miami-heat-lebron-james-s061112_1_heat-teammate-dwyane-wade-lebron-james-media-day

CHAPTER 5—HAVE YOUR TEAMMATE'S BACK

Yogi Berra—*When You Come to a Fork in the Road, Take It!: Inspiration and Wisdom from One of Baseball's Greatest Heroes* (2001)

Simon Sinek—https://twitter.com/simonsinek/status/232556392114974721?lang=en

T.J. McConnell—https://www.youtube.com/watch?v=nQX4klW8snE

Bob Ladouceur—http://www.spartanhood.com/whatisaspartan.htm

Mike Krzyzewski—*The Gold Standard: Building a World-Class Team* (2009)

Terry Francona—http://abcnews.go.com/Sports/mike-aviles-teams-gesture-means-lot/story?id=31373595

Bobby Bowden—*Called to Coach: Reflections on Life, Faith and Football* (2011)

CHAPTER 6—KEEP YOUR COMMITMENTS AND DELIVER RESULTS

Message to Garcia Story—http://www.foundationsmag.com/rowan.html

Elbert Hubbard—http://www.foundationsmag.com/rowan.html

Maya Angelou—*Rainbow in the Cloud: The Wisdom and Spirit of Maya Angelou* (2014)

Dean Oliver—*Basketball on Paper: Rules and Tools for Performance Analysis* (2003)

Shaka Smart—http://sayquotable.com/quotes/quote-about-players-think-play-me-and-ill-show-you-coache-image.html

Alex Morgan—https://www.womenshealthmag.com/fitness/olympic-soccer-star-alex-morgan

Brad Stevens—https://www.bostonglobe.com/sports/2016/01/07/brad-stevens-philosophy-loose-balls-floor/CwofnhiVqW4UodiOH4qGeK/story.html

PHOTO CREDITS

Page v—Anson Dorrance and Jeff Janssen—courtesy of Jeff Janssen

Page viii—Bev Smith courtesy of South Carolina Athletics media relations.

Page xv—Luke Waechter courtesy of Charlotte Athletics media relations.

Page xvi—Ciara Gregory courtesy of Charlotte Athletics media relations.

Page xxvi—Joe Beery and Andrew Townes courtesy of Stetson Athletics media relations.

Page xxvii—Dylan Bell courtesy of StFX Athletics media relations.

Page 9—Darcy McFarlane courtesy of Shane Lardinois.

Page 18—Allison LaBeau courtesy of Lehigh Athletics media relations.

Page 29—Julian Plummer courtesy of Lafayette Athletics media relations.

Page 32—Tommy Yanchus courtesy of Guelph Athletics media relations.

Page 38—Maddy Stover courtesy of Utah Athletics media relations.

Page 46—Danielle Burns courtesy of Fordham Athletics media relations.

Page 50—Calvin Hawke courtesy of Barton Athletics media relations.

Page 58—Maggie Skjelbred courtesy of Stetson Athletics media relations.

Page 64—Michael Clarke courtesy of StFX Athletics media relations.

Page 66—Jet Manzi courtesy of Lafayette Athletics media relations.

Page 70—Jillian Janssen courtesy of Jeff Janssen.

Page 86—Megan Zimlich courtesy of Robert Black and Arkansas media relations.

Page 94—Amanda Magadan courtesy of Lafayette Athletics media relations.

Page 100—Estelle Wong courtesy of Fordham Athletics media relations.

Page 102—Cameron Critchlow courtesy of UNB Athletics media relations.

Page 108—Haley Pace courtesy of Charlotte Athletics media relations.

Page 113—Brittany Florjancic courtesy of UNB Athletics media relations.

JANSSEN SPORTS LEADERSHIP CENTER PROGRAMS

HOW TO BUILD AND SUSTAIN A CHAMPIONSHIP CULTURE

Want to build a Championship Culture in your program? This dynamic workshop shows coaches and captains the secrets of building and sustaining a winning culture. Learn how to create a Clear and Compelling Vision for your team, develop your Core Values, determine your Standards of Behavior, enhance your team's Commitment and Unity, and align your program's Systems for maximum impact.

LEADERSHIP SUMMIT

Our highly engaging and interactive Leadership Summit teaches your athletes the sports leadership skills and strategies necessary to be strong and effective leaders for your team. Based on our world-famous Sports Leadership Academies at top colleges across the nation, your student-athletes can learn some of the same sports leadership skills taught at high-level programs.

The 75-minute Leadership Summit is an interactive workshop designed for emerging and existing student-athlete leaders at the college, high school, or club level. The program also includes a dedicated 75-minute workshop for coaches on how best to develop, select, and partner with your leaders.

LEADERSHIP RETREAT

The more intensive Leadership Retreat includes up to six hours of advanced leadership training for student-athletes and coaches conducted in a fun and fast-paced environment. The programming targets two separate student-athlete groups, Emerging Leaders and Veteran Leaders, based on their readiness to assume leadership roles. We also provide an advanced leadership workshop for the coaching staff.

Plus, to reinforce and extend the programming throughout the year, the participants also receive a copy of *The Team Captain's Leadership Manual* and a year-long membership to the online TeamCaptainsNetwok.com. The Leadership Retreat makes a great early season option to provide your leaders with the knowledge and skills they'll need to step up and lead throughout the season.

LEADERSHIP ACADEMY

The comprehensive Leadership Academy provides your athletic department with an ongoing and integrated approach to leadership development by targeting and training three distinct groups of leaders (Emerging Leaders, Veteran Leaders, Leadership 360) and distributes the training with multiple modules offered throughout the school year to maximize learning, retention, and application.

In addition to the programming, the Leadership Academy also includes educational resources for all participants to reinforce and extend the learning as well as an ongoing consulting retainer with the Janssen Sports Leadership Center for advice and trouble-shooting various issues that arise throughout the year.

For more info on the Janssen Sports Leadership Center visit
www.JanssenSportsLeadership.com

SPORTS LEADERSHIP DEVELOPMENT SERIES

Our popular Sports Leadership Development Series provides athletes, coaches, and athletic administrators with a practical, progressive, and proven sports leadership development training program that spans a student-athlete's entire career. The comprehensive curriculum targets student-athletes at their specific level of leadership development. The series starts with teaching the critical self leadership skills of responsibility, accountability, and commitment and then progresses on to the more advanced skills of effective team leadership building a championship culture, and holding teammates accountable. So no matter where your athletes might be in terms of their personal leadership development, you'll have the appropriate level of training for them.

Level 1: Personal Responsibility—*The Athlete's Responsibility Manual*
The Athlete's Responsibility Manual trains student-athletes how to take full responsibility for themselves by owning their choices, decisions, and actions. The six-module program is geared for all freshmen to complete as early as possible during their first year—or as a great summer read before they start school.

Level 2: Team Accountability—*The Teammate's Accountability Manual*
The Teammate's Accountability Manual shows athletes how their attitudes and actions significantly impact their teammates' and coaches' success and failure. This six-module program extends and expands on the material in Level 1 and can be done with all freshmen in the first semester of their first year.

Level 3: Commitment—*The Athlete's Commitment Manual*
The Athlete's Commitment Manual trains student-athletes how to completely commit to their task, training, and team through the use of the powerful Commitment Continuum™ tool. This six-module program can be done with all freshmen in the second semester of their first year.

Level 4: Team Leadership—*The Team Captain's Leadership Manual*
Designed for emerging team leaders, *The Team Captain's Leadership Manual* is a 10-module leadership development program that trains athletes how to be effective Leaders by Example and Vocal Leaders. Use it early on with your sophomores who demonstrate leadership potential.

Level 5: Championship Culture—*The Team Captain's Culture Manual*
Designed for established team leaders, *The Team Captain's Culture Manual* teaches captains how to best partner with the coaches to build and sustain a Championship Culture in your program. Use this 10-module, advanced leadership development program with your junior and senior team captains.

Level 6: Holding People Accountable—*How to Hold People Accountable Manual*
Designed for respected team leaders, the *How to Hold People Accountable Manual* teaches and trains your leaders how to effectively hold their teammates accountable to your team's standards and core values. Use this 8-module, advanced program with your senior team leaders.

For more info on the Janssen Sports Leadership Center visit
www.JanssenSportsLeadership.com

HOW TO BE AN ACCOUNTABLE TEAMMATE

ACCOUNTABLE ATHLETE

Keep Your Commitments and Deliver Results

Own Your Responsibilities and Role

Have Your Teammate's Back

Recognize Your Ripple Effect

EXCUSES

Eliminate Excuses

Consider the Consequences

Accountable 2U

© JanssenSportsLeadership.com